SAUCES & SALSAS

SAUCES & SALSAS

Oded Schwartz

Photography by Ian O'Leary

DK PUBLISHING, Inc.

www.dk.com

A DK PUBLISHING BOOK

Project Editor Nasim Mawji

Art Editor Sue Storey
at Patrick McLeavy & Partners

Senior Editor Jane Middleton

Senior Art Editor Tracey Ward

DTP Designer Bridget Roseberry

Managing Editor Susannah Marriott

Deputy Art Director Carole Ash

Managing Art Editor Toni Kay

Production Controller Sarah Coltman

Food Stylists Alison Austin,
Jane Suthering, and Oded Schwartz

US Editor Barbara Minton

*This book is for Vicki McIvor, my agent and my friend.
Without her encouragement, trust and dedication my work
would have been impossible.*

All recipes serve 4–6 unless otherwise indicated

Some recipes in this book contain raw eggs. Because of the
risk of salmonella poisoning, young children, the elderly,
pregnant women, and those with impaired immune
systems should avoid raw eggs.

Preserving and canning are not without their risks. The procedures described in this
book should be taken only as general guidelines; for more specific information, contact
your agricultural extension agent. For canning, use USDA-approved jars and sealants only;
many of the jars shown here are intended for illustration purposes only and are not
appropriate for heat processing or long-term storage. DK Publishing assumes no
responsibility for illness or injury resulting from the use of this book.

First American Edition, 1999
2 4 6 8 10 9 7 5 3 1

Published in the United States by DK Publishing, Inc.,
95 Madison Avenue, New York, New York 10016
www.dk.com

Library of Congress Catagloging-in-Publication Data
Schwartz, Oded.
Sauces and Salsas / by Oded Schwartz. -- 1st American ed.
p.   cm.
Includes index.
ISBN 0-7894-4627-8 (alk. paper)
1. Sauces.   2. Salsas (Cookery)   I. Title.
TX819.S29S38   1999
641.8' 14--dc21   99-14526
                                   CIP

Reproduced in Singapore by Colourscan
Printed and bound in Spain by Artes Gráficas Toledo S.A.U.
D.L. TO: 1260 - 1999

CONTENTS

INTRODUCTION

THERE IS NO SORCERY INVOLVED IN MAKING A GOOD SAUCE — all you need are fresh ingredients, simple techniques, a bit of patience, and a dash of imagination.

From the simple sauces of ancient civilizations – mixtures of vinegar, salt, and oils – to the elegant, rich concoctions of classic French cuisine, sauces have always played an important part in cooking. Recently, though, they have fallen out of favor with home cooks, who tend to think that they are fussy and time-consuming to prepare as well as rich and full of calories. This book takes a new approach and aims to show that sauces can be light, fresh, and quick to make. It provides step-by-step advice on classic techniques – for béchamel, Hollandaise, beurre blanc, sabayon, and coulis, for example – and also includes a huge range of modern sauces and relishes.

In response to our increasingly adventurous palates, our hectic lifestyles, and our considerably healthier eating habits, here are sauces in the broadest sense of the word. Salsas – combinations of finely chopped fresh fruit and vegetables that require no cooking at all – can enliven a piece of broiled chicken or fish. Fresh dips can be served as part of a mezze or eaten as a light snack. Dressings can be drizzled over a bowl of crisp leaves. Coconut chutney will transform a simple samosa. I have also included an international selection of hearty and warming cooking sauces, many of which can be left to cook slowly and form an integral part of a dish.

Whether it is a rich Hollandaise, a spoonful of spicy paste, a spread of flavored butter, a freshly prepared relish, or a zesty marinade, a well-made sauce can elevate simple ingredients to the sublime. Sauces add moisture, flavor, color and texture to food. They are also very versatile. Many of the intensely flavored pastes and relishes can be mixed with cream cheese, yogurt, or mayonnaise to make delicious dips and dressings, or spooned over pasta, polenta, couscous, or rice for a light meal. Plain sauces can be vehicles for many different flavorings if you vary your choice of herbs and spices. Use your imagination and experiment.

Happily, the days when sauces were regarded with suspicion as a means for concealing poor-quality ingredients are long gone. These days sauces are invariably the crowning glory of a dish. A carefully chosen sauce will perfectly complement the ingredients you are serving it with, highlighting and harmonizing flavors without dominating. The trick is to understand the versatility of sauces and to be imaginative in the way that you serve them. I have included a chart at the end of the book (see Matching Sauces with Food, pages 138–40), to help you partner sauces with appropriate ingredients.

Sauces & Salsas is an eclectic collection of my favorite recipes. Rich, spicy, subtle, or delicate, time-honored or created especially for this book, these recipes represent a fascinating culinary trip round the world. Be saucy with your sauces, and use this book as a guide – a blueprint for new ways of cooking. I hope that it will inspire you to create your own new and exciting sauces and salsas and that you enjoy using it as much as I have enjoyed writing it.

A Gallery of Sauces

This tantalizing gallery will help

you turn fresh and exciting

ingredients into delicious and

appetizing sauces, salsas, marinades,

and relishes. Use this inspirational

collection of ingredients and ideas

to expand your culinary repertoire.

HERB SAUCES

HERBS & THEIR USES

✦ BAY
Used to flavor stocks, sauces, and stews; a pungent leaf which should be used fresh or in small quantities dried.

✦ ROSEMARY
Essential in Mediterranean cooking; good with meat, fish, and vegetables. Use fresh or dried, but dried tends to be bitter so use it sparingly.

✦ SAGE
Pungent so use only in small quantities so the flavor won't be overwhelming; there are several varieties, all have a real affinity for meat. The leaves have a soft down.

✦ BASIL
Sweet and superbly fragrant, basil is a classic herb to serve with tomatoes. We think of basil as an Italian herb, but it is just as important in Thai cooking.

✦ TARRAGON
A pungent herb with a complex flavor; it has a real affinity for fish and white meat, such as chicken or veal. Important for flavoring vinegar and many sauces.

✦ PARSLEY
A versatile favorite; the flat-leaf variety has a stronger, fresher flavor. Always use fresh.

✦ OREGANO
A favorite Mediterranean herb that has a great affinity for tomatoes as well as lamb and chicken. Used both fresh and dried.

✦ DILL
Fresh-tasting and fragrant with a subtle flavor of anise. Use with fish, chicken, or vegetables. Use fresh.

✦ MINT
There are several varieties of this fresh-tasting herb. Popular in sauces and excellent with lamb, chicken, legumes, vegetables, and fruit.

FRESH, FRAGRANT, AND FULL OF FLAVOR, HERBS ARE ESSENTIAL TO GOOD COOKING. HERBS WITH TOUGH LEAVES, SUCH AS THYME, BAY, AND ROSEMARY, HAVE A STRONG TASTE AND SHOULD BE USED SPARINGLY OTHERWISE THEY CAN OVERPOWER SAUCES AND GIVE A BITTER FLAVOR. LONG, SLOW COOKING CAN ALTER AN HERB'S FLAVOR — ADDING A SMALL AMOUNT OF THE FRESH HERB JUST BEFORE SERVING CAN REVITALIZE IT. TO KEEP HERBS FRESH, SNIP OFF THE DRY ENDS OF THE STEMS AND EITHER STAND IN A JAR OF FRESH WATER OR WRAP THE STEMS IN DAMP PAPER TOWELS AND STORE IN A PLASTIC BAG IN THE VEGETABLE DRAWER OF THE REFRIGERATOR. IN GENERAL, FRESH HERBS ARE BETTER THAN DRIED FOR SAUCES, BUT DRIED HERBS HAVE THEIR USES, SUCH AS IN MARINADES AND SPICE PASTES.

ROSEMARY OIL

MAIN IMAGE: rosemary-infused oil drizzled over thin slices of smoked halibut makes an elegant hors d'oeuvre. (*See page 70*)

DILL PESTO

TOP: try dill pesto on polenta topped with broiled red pepper, red onion, and shavings of Parmesan. (*See page 120*)

GREEN GODDESS DRESSING

MIDDLE: parsley-flecked green goddess dressing is the perfect accompaniment to a juicy fillet steak. (*See page 72*)

MEDITERRANEAN MARINADE

BOTTOM: swordfish steaks absorb the fresh flavors of a zesty, Mediterranean dill and parsley marinade. (*See page 108*)

SPICES & AROMATICS & THEIR USES

✦ LEMONGRASS
The thickened stem of a wild grass native to Southeast Asia, this has a lemony flavor and a delicious perfumed aroma.

✦ CINNAMON
The aromatic bark of a tree; available as quills, bark chips, or ground. Used in sweet and savory cooking.

✦ CASSIA
A close relative of cinnamon, more commonly used in savory cooking since it is coarser in flavor. Often used in Indian curries.

✦ VANILLA
The fragrant seed pod of a tropical orchid; the fresh bean has a superior, more subtle flavor than vanilla extract. Natural vanilla extract is a better substitute than vanilla essence.

✦ KAFFIR LIME LEAVES
The fragrant leaves of the kaffir lime tree give a distinctive fresh lemon flavor to many Southeast Asian dishes. Used fresh or dried; the fresh leaves freeze well.

✦ TAMARIND
The pod of the tamarind tree; available in block form or as a dark paste, it is soaked in warm water to give a fruity, sweet-sour-flavored liquid popular in Indian and Southeast Asian cooking.

✦ GINGER
This root has been cultivated in tropical Asia for over 3,000 years. Hot, warming, and slightly sweet in flavor, it is best used fresh, but is also available dried, ground, and pickled.

✦ GALANGAL
The highly aromatic rhizomes of a tropical plant. Although interchangeable with ginger, galangal has a stronger, more camphorated flavor much loved in Malay and Thai cooking.

SAUCES USING SPICES & AROMATICS

JUST AS A PAINTER USES COLOR TO ADD SUBTLE NUANCES, A COOK USES SPICES AND AROMATICS TO INTRODUCE DELICATE FLAVORS AND AROMAS TO MANY SAUCES. THE RANGE OF SPICES AND AROMATICS POPULARLY USED IS CONSTANTLY EXPANDING AS MORE EXOTIC INGREDIENTS BECOME WIDELY AVAILABLE. AROMATICS SHOULD BE USED SPARINGLY; MANY ARE QUITE BITTER AND STRONG IN FLAVOR AND CAN OVERWHELM. BUY SPICES AND AROMATICS IN SMALL QUANTITIES AND STORE IN TIGHTLY CLOSED CONTAINERS — EXPOSURE TO AIR WILL CAUSE THE AROMA TO FADE. IF POSSIBLE, FREEZE THEM TO CAPTURE THEIR FRESHNESS.

LEMONGRASS BUTTER SAUCE

MAIN IMAGE: juicy morsels of chicken on a lemongrass skewer with a velvety-smooth aromatic butter sauce. (*See page 54*)

TAMARIND DIPPING SAUCE

TOP: tart and fruity and speckled with spring onions and cilantro, this light sauce is perfect for dipping delicate filo parcels. (*See page 125*)

SOSATIE

MIDDLE: lamb cutlets in a traditional South African sauce with tamarind, lemon leaves, and ginger. (*See page 113*)

EXOTIC FRUIT RELISH

BOTTOM: a sweet concoction of pineapple, aromatic ginger, and kaffir lime leaves served with salmon. (*See page 103*)

CHILIES & THEIR USES

✦ **ANAHEIM (CHILI VERDE)**
Common in the US; also known as California Long. Green, but can be red. Mild.

✦ **CASCABEL (JINGLE BELL)**
Deep red in color; used fresh or dried. Mild.

✦ **BIRD'S EYE (THAI: PRIK KII NOO SUAN)**
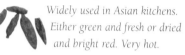
Widely used in Asian kitchens. Either green and fresh or dried and bright red. Very hot.

✦ **CAYENNE (HADES HOT)**
Essential in Creole and Cajun cooking; the original component of cayenne pepper. Very hot.

✦ **SANTA FE GRANDE (CARIBE, CALORO, OR GOLD SPIKE)**
Yellow, orange, or red, and used fresh or dried, whole or powdered. Mild to moderate.

✦ **CHORICERO**
An important ingredient in Spanish chorizo; a big chili, used both fresh and dried. Mild.

✦ **GUAJILLO**
A Mexican chili favored for its delicate flavor and russet-red coloring. Mild.

✦ **FRESNO**
Light green, ripening to cherry red; used fresh. Hot.

✦ **JALAPEÑO/CHIPOTLE**
Chipotles are smoke-dried jalapeños and have a smoky flavor. Hot.

✦ **PASILLA**
Called 'little raisin' in Spanish because of its dried, wrinkled pods and raisin-like aroma; used in stews. Mild to moderate.

✦ **HABANERO (SCOTCH BONNET)**
Intensely flavored; important in Caribbean cooking. Very hot.

✦ **SERRANO**
Green, red, or orange; used fresh. Hot.

CHILI SAUCES

FRESH, DRIED, HOT, SWEET, OR MILD, CHILIES PLAY AN ESSENTIAL ROLE IN THE GLOBAL KITCHEN, ADDING FLAVOR, TEXTURE, AND A BRIGHT, APPETIZING COLOR TO SAUCES FROM EVERY CONTINENT. LIKE TOMATOES, CHILIES WERE INTRODUCED TO THE OLD WORLD FROM THE AMERICAS, WHERE THEY GREW WILD. THEY ARE HIGH IN VITAMINS C AND A, AND IN CAPSAICIN, THE SOURCE OF THEIR HEAT. THE HEAT OF A CHILI VARIES ACCORDING TO THE TYPE USED. VERY HOT CHILIES CAN CAUSE A PAINFUL BURNING SENSATION IF BROUGHT INTO CONTACT WITH EYES OR SENSITIVE SKIN; IT IS ADVISABLE TO WEAR GLOVES WHEN HANDLING THEM. EXERCISE CAUTION AS WELL, WHEN COOKING WITH CHILIES, GRADUALLY EXPERIMENTING WITH THE MANY TYPES AND BUILDING UP YOUR PERSONAL TOLERANCE LEVEL.

TOMATO & CHILI SAUCE

MAIN IMAGE: a tangy, chili-spiked tomato sauce elevates lightly broiled haddock fillet to gourmet status. (*See page 76*)

THAI DIPPING SAUCE

TOP: an Oriental-style sauce laced with thin slices of chili makes the perfect accompaniment to shrimp. (*See page 125*)

HARISSA

MIDDLE: a versatile chili sauce that adds instant piquancy to soups, stews, sauces, and even mayonnaise. (*See page 103*)

POMEGRANATE SALSA

BOTTOM: chili, pomegranate seeds, and cilantro are combined in this vibrantly colored salsa. (*See page 97*)

TOMATOES & THEIR USES

✦ BEEFSTEAK TOMATOES
These are large, juicy, firm-fleshed, and easy to peel; a versatile tomato suitable for salsas, salads, and stuffing.

✦ COLORED TOMATOES
Yellow, orange, purple, and striped tomatoes are now readily available. Use these when a different colored sauce is needed.

✦ CHERRY TOMATOES
Bite-sized and sweet-fleshed, these tomatoes are delicious fresh or cooked; like all tomatoes, the vine-ripened variety are more flavorful.

✦ SUN-DRIED TOMATOES
The raisins of the savory kitchen, these are usually plum tomatoes cured with salt and dried in the sun; available dried (which need soaking in water before use) or hydrated and preserved in oil. Intensely flavored, they can be used in small quantities.

✦ TOMATO PASTE
A smooth concentrated purée of strained cooked tomatoes. Widely used to add rich color and enhance the flavor of cooked tomato dishes. Commercially produced and sold in cans, but also easy to prepare at home.

✦ CANNED TOMATOES
A convenient alternative to fresh tomatoes. When using, drain off the liquid and gently squeeze out any excess moisture. A standard 15oz (450g) can of tomatoes, drained and squeezed, will replace ½lb (250g) fresh tomatoes. Plum tomatoes are most commonly canned, but cherry tomatoes are also available.

TOMATO SAUCES

JUICY AND IRRESISTIBLY SWEET-FLESHED, TOMATOES ARE AN INDISPENSABLE INGREDIENT. LIKE CHILIES, THEY WERE INTRODUCED TO THE OLD WORLD FROM THE AMERICAS IN THE 16TH CENTURY. HOWEVER, IT WAS ONLY WHEN THE ITALIANS EMBRACED TOMATOES WITH SUCH ENTHUSIASM IN THE 19TH CENTURY THAT THEY BECAME UNIVERSALLY POPULAR. NOW ALL SORTS OF DIFFERENT VARIETIES OF TOMATO ARE AVAILABLE: THE BEST HAVE A SUPERB AROMA AND A DELICATE SWEET AND SOUR BALANCE, PERFECT FOR MAKING SAUCES AND SALSAS. COOKING CONCENTRATES THEIR FLAVOR, AND, USED FRESH, THEY ADD MOISTURE AND FRUITINESS TO MANY DISHES. TOMATOES CONTAIN CAROTENOIDS, PROVEN CANCER FIGHTERS, WHICH GIVE THEM THEIR RED COLOR. AVOID USING WATERY SALAD TOMATOES.

FRESH TOMATO COULIS

MAIN IMAGE: the perfect filling for a ripe avocado served with crunchy tortilla chips. (*See page 59*)

TOMATO GRAVY

TOP: fresh tomato paste and sun-dried tomatoes add a wonderful tanginess to traditional pan gravy. (*See page 65*)

TWO-TOMATO RELISH

MIDDLE: sweet-fleshed cherry tomatoes and sun-dried tomatoes in a relish that marries well with chicken. (*See page 103*)

TOMATO RAITA

BOTTOM: plum tomatoes and yogurt are partnered in this cooling, fragrant sauce, perfect with a hot curry. (*See page 104*)

DAIRY PRODUCTS & THEIR USES

◆ MILK
Although many people consider skim or one percent milk the healthy option, most sauces need the rich, smooth texture of whole milk.

◆ LIGHT CREAM
Contains 18–20 percent butter fat. Suitable for pouring but not for whipping.

◆ HEAVY CREAM
Smooth and rich, with a minimum of 48 percent fat; the most useful cream in sauce-making. Suitable for whipping.

◆ CRÈME FRAÎCHE
Heavy cream treated with a culture to give a light acidity without sourness.

◆ SOUR CREAM
Contains 16–40 percent fat; smooth, fresh, and mildly acidic in flavor. A popular base for dressings and dips.

◆ YOGURT
Milk soured by the addition of bacteria. Varieties contain 0–10 percent fat and are creamy in texture with a tart flavor. Makes a good low-fat alternative to cream.

◆ BLUE CHEESES
Cheeses, such as gorgonzola, Stilton, and Danish blue, with 30–60 percent fat, add pungency to many sauces.

◆ FRESH WHITE CHEESES
Skim milk curd cheeses are very low in fat; cream cheese contains about 47 percent fat. They are used mainly as bases for dips and spreads.

◆ HARD & SEMI-HARD CHEESES
Italian Parmesan, Pecorino (made from sheep's milk), and Cheddar contain 30–60 percent fat. Easy to grate, they are the most commonly used cheeses for cooking.

◆ BUTTER
Made from cream skimmed from milk and then churned; use a good-quality unsalted variety when cooking.

DAIRY SAUCES

MILK, CREAM, BUTTER, YOGURT, AND CHEESE ARE THE FOUNDATIONS OF MANY SAUCES. WHAT COULD BE SIMPLER THAN A SAUCE MADE OF MELTED BUTTER, ENLIVENED WITH A FEW DROPS OF LEMON JUICE? OR SMOOTH CREAM OR YOGURT FLAVORED WITH A FEW CAREFULLY CHOSEN FRESH HERBS OR SPICES? MILK IS THE BASIS FOR COMFORTING WHITE SAUCES AND CUSTARDS. CREAM ADDS RICHNESS AND A VELVETY TEXTURE, WHILE SOUR CREAM, CRÈME FRAÎCHE, AND YOGURT LEND SMOOTHNESS, FRESHNESS, AND A PLEASANT TARTNESS. CHEESE GIVES FLAVOR AND TEXTURE AND ADDS AN APPETIZING GOLDEN CRUST TO GRATIN DISHES; BLUE CHEESE GIVES AN UNUSUAL PIQUANCY TO DRESSINGS AND SAUCES. FOR THE BEST FLAVOR, BUY THE BEST QUALITY CHEESE YOU CAN FIND.

TANDOORI MARINADE

MAIN IMAGE: tandoori poussin and naan. Yogurt in the marinade lends subtlety to the delicate flavors. (*See page 110*)

YOGURT & HONEY SAUCE

TOP: succulent figs with honey-marbled yogurt and fresh mint make a light and healthy dessert. (*See page 128*)

CHOCOLATE CUSTARD

MIDDLE: a caramelized orange topped with orange peel sits in a puddle of rich, smooth chocolate custard. (*See page 126*)

MORNAY SAUCE

BOTTOM: broccoli in a cheese Mornay sauce, lightly broiled to give a slightly crunchy, golden topping. (*See page 49*)

FRUIT & ITS USES

✦ APPLES
For sauce-making, use tart cooking apples such as McIntosh, which cook down to a smooth pulp. Eating apples, such as Granny Smith, tend to hold their shape when cooked.

✦ BERRIES
Brightly colored and sweet and sour in flavor, berries cook well and are very useful for adding attractive color. Redcurrants are used in Cumberland sauce; cranberry sauce is the traditional accompaniment to roast turkey.

✦ FRUIT WITH PITS
Ripe cherries, plums, peaches, and nectarines make good bases for sweet and savory sauces.

✦ CITRUS FRUITS
Lemons, limes, and oranges add tangy flavor. Enhance the citrus flavor in sauces by adding grated peel. The juice of lemons and limes contains vitamin C, which helps prevent avocados and some fruits from discoloring.

✦ TROPICAL FRUITS
Enzymes in papayas tenderize tough meat; mangoes are delicious in salsas and chutneys; pineapples are popular in chutneys and are also used in meat-tenderizing marinades. Popular for adding exotic flavors – especially to dessert sauces.

✦ BANANAS
Sprinkling peeled bananas with lemon or lime juice prevents discoloration. Starchy and high in potassium, they are used to thicken and add flavor to many Mexican, Southeast Asian, and Indian sauces.

✦ POMEGRANATES
One of the most ancient fruits, indigenous to Persia; edible seeds are encased in juicy, red flesh. A popular ingredient in Middle Eastern cooking; also good in salsas.

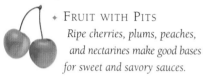

FRUIT SAUCES

USE FRESH FRUIT IN COULIS AND DESSERT SAUCES OR AS AN UNUSUAL AND TANGY ADDITION TO SALSAS. COOKED FRUITS SUCH AS BERRIES, APPLES, AND CHERRIES ARE SERVED AS ACCOMPANIMENTS TO ROAST MEAT AND POULTRY. FRUIT SAUCES CUT THE RICHNESS OF FATTY MEATS, SUCH AS DUCK AND PORK, AND SUCH FISH AS MACKEREL OR SALMON. APPLES, PEARS, AND QUINCES, WHICH CONTAIN LARGE AMOUNTS OF PECTIN, ARE USED TO THICKEN AND ADD SWEETNESS AND TEXTURE TO SAUCES. CITRUS FRUITS WITH THEIR FRESH FLAVOR, ARE UNIVERSALLY USED TO ENLIVEN SAUCES; THEY ARE ALSO RICH IN VITAMIN C, NATURE'S BEST ANTIOXIDANT. WHEN CHOOSING FRUIT, CHECK FOR SOFT SPOTS OR BRUISES AND, UNLESS YOU PLAN TO EAT THE FRUIT IMMEDIATELY, BUY PRODUCE THAT IS SLIGHTLY UNDERRIPE AND RIPEN IT AT HOME IN YOUR FRUIT BASKET.

BANANA CARAMEL SAUCE

MAIN IMAGE: a rich and luxurious blend of bananas, fresh cream, and caramel poured over a tower of hot pancakes. (*See page 129*)

BEET & APPLE SALSA

TOP: creamy goat cheese on a croûte base with a tangy beet and apple salsa and a scattering of red chard. (*See page 96*)

CHERRY SAUCE

MIDDLE: try tart and fresh cherry sauce spooned over a slice of ham and lightly sautéed potatoes. (*See page 118*)

RASPBERRY VINAIGRETTE

BOTTOM: juicy slices of duck on a bed of mixed leaves drizzled with ruby-colored fresh raspberry vinaigrette. (*See page 69*)

ALCOHOL & ITS USES

✦ SPIRITS AGED IN GLASS
A large family of pure alcohol usually distilled from fermented fruit, starch, and grains. Varieties include kirsch, framboise, and fraises de bois. Others such as grappa, eau de vie, and vodka are flavorless and are used mainly for their high alcohol content.

✦ SPIRITS AGED IN WOOD
Probably the most widely used flavoring agents in the kitchen, this group includes cognac, whisky, brandy, Calvados, and rum. Matured in aged wood, these robust and strong-flavored alcohols are used in small quantities to add a kick to sweet and savory sauces.

✦ FORTIFIED WINES
Both sweet and dry, these are a mixture of aged wines, sometimes aromatized, and different grape brandies that are fortified with the addition of a spirit. This group, including sherries, Madeira, port, marsala, and rice wine, add sweetness and a delicate, slightly aromatic flavor.

✦ FRUIT-FLAVORED LIQUEURS
A large family of blended liqueurs flavored with different fruit juices, peels, oils, and leaves. These include Grand Marnier, triple sec, Curaçao, Cointreau, cherry brandy, and apricot, banana, and pineapple liqueurs, among many more. They are used to impart sweetness and a good fruity aroma.

✦ ALCOHOL FLAVORED WITH AROMATICS
Alcohol that has had spices and aromatics such as coffee, vanilla, cloves, bitters, herbs, peels, or wood chips added to it and is then either filtered or distilled to capture the flavor – Pernod, arak, and ouzo, for example. Although mainly used as apéritifs and digestifs, they can be used to flavor a variety of sauces.

ALCOHOLIC SAUCES

WINES, SPIRITS, AND FORTIFIED LIQUEURS ARE INCLUDED IN MANY SAUCES. RED WINE GIVES A MORE ROBUST FLAVOR THAN WHITE WINE. IT IS IMPORTANT TO REDUCE WINE WELL AFTER ADDING IT TO A SAUCE – WHEN ALCOHOL EVAPORATES, THE FLAVORS CONCENTRATE AND MELLOW. CHAMPAGNE LIGHTENS SAUCES, WHILE LIQUEURS MADE WITH FRUIT, HERBS, AND FORTIFIED WINES, SUCH AS SHERRY, RICE WINE, OR MADEIRA, ARE USED TO GIVE FLAVOR AND AROMA. THEY ARE GENERALLY ADDED IN SMALL QUANTITIES TOWARD THE END OF COOKING. FRUIT-FLAVORED LIQUEURS WILL BOOST THE TASTE OF FRESH FRUIT SAUCES – COINTREAU IS DELICIOUS IN AN ORANGE SAUCE, FOR EXAMPLE. DON'T BE TEMPTED TO COOK WITH CHEAP WINES AND LIQUEURS: THEY PRODUCE COARSE AND THIN-TASTING RESULTS.

ZABAGLIONE

MAIN IMAGE: a classic Italian dessert, zabaglione is creamy, frothy, and spiked with sweet marsala wine. (*See page 128*)

COOKED VINAIGRETTE

TOP: a light orange and chicory salad drizzled with a fragrant vinaigrette laced with white wine. (*See page 69*)

RUM & GINGER BUTTER

MIDDLE: butter, rum, and stem ginger being beaten together until light and creamy. (*See page 133*)

JUNIPER DEMI-GLAZE

BOTTOM: red wine and gin give a robust flavor to this demi-glaze served with medallions of pork and kale. (*See page 61*)

TECHNIQUES

MAKING SAUCES IS NOT DIFFICULT — THEY

DO NOT REQUIRE COMPLICATED SKILLS

OR SPECIALIZED EQUIPMENT. TAKE TIME TO

MASTER A FEW SIMPLE TECHNIQUES; NOT

ONLY WILL THEY ENSURE ROBUSTLY

FLAVORED STOCKS, FROTHY SABAYONS,

AND GLOSSY MAYONNAISES, BUT THEY

WILL PROVIDE THE FOUNDATIONS ON WHICH

TO EXPERIMENT AND DEVELOP SAUCES

OF YOUR OWN.

EQUIPMENT

YOU DO NOT NEED SPECIALIZED EQUIPMENT to make a successful sauce. The tools shown here can be found in any reasonably well-stocked kitchen. When purchasing new kitchen equipment, always buy the best because it will last longer. Choose equipment that feels comfortable in your hand and that is made from a noncorrosive material, such as stainless steel, plastic, or glass, which will not react with acidic foods.

Flat whisks or beaters: enable you to reach the corners of a pan.

Balloon whisks: suitable for whisking in bowls.

Flat-coiled wire beaters: convenient for use in bowls and pans.

BOWL PLACED OVER A SAUCEPAN
An easy-to-assemble substitute for a double boiler, this provides a gentle way of cooking and heating sauces, especially Hollandaise, sabayon, and custard. Make sure that the bottom of the bowl does not touch the simmering water in the pan.

SAUCEPANS
Always choose heavy-bottomed saucepans because they conduct heat more evenly, enabling better temperature control.

WHISKS OR BEATERS
Good for mixing and combining liquid ingredients and introducing air into a sauce, making it lighter in consistency. Select a whisk that feels comfortable and is the right weight and shape for your hand. Always buy them in noncorrosive stainless steel.

MORTAR AND PESTLE
A traditional instrument for pounding ingredients into pastes and purées – a method that retains the full flavor and gives a texture that cannot be matched by food processors.

ELECTRICAL EQUIPMENT

Electric stand mixer: makes it easy to whisk mayonnaise and to beat eggs, cream, and butters – especially when making large quantities. For smaller quantities, use a hand-held beater.

Hand blender: convenient for puréeing in pans or for puréeing small quantities.

BLENDER

ELECTRIC STAND MIXER

HAND BLENDER

SPICE MILL

FOOD PROCESSOR

Blender: ideal for puréeing to a smooth, fine consistency.

Food processor: good for mixing, coarse chopping, and puréeing; its obvious advantage is its speed, though some argue that this can compromise flavor.

Spice mill: used for pulverizing and grinding spices. Commercially produced spice powders are finer but spices freshly ground in a spice mill are always more flavorful.

STRAINERS

These are often essential for achieving a smooth consistency and for rescuing lumpy sauces. Both conical and round ones are available, and all vary in fineness of mesh. Have at least two sizes in your kitchen: a larger one for straining stocks and a smaller one for straining sauces or puréeing. Clean them under running water then shake or tap to free water trapped in the mesh.

GRATER

This is a convenient little instrument for scraping the zest from citrus fruit or for grating cheese.

SKIMMERS

Useful for removing residue that collects on the surface of stocks and simmering sauces; always keep a bowl of cold water nearby to rinse the skimmer between liftings.

LEMON SQUEEZER

Designed to fit the shape of a halved lemon, it can also be used for juicing oranges and for straining the seeds from the juice.

CHICKEN STOCK

NO BOUILLON CUBE CAN BE COMPARED with a homemade stock prepared from fresh ingredients. Because stock is the basis of so many dishes, preparing it yourself is greatly worthwhile. You can also be creative by flavoring your stock according to the dishes it is intended for. The perfect chicken stock is light in color and clear, which you can achieve by using mature stewing hens, preferably free-range and organic. Bones from young roasting chickens will not do – they do not contain enough flavor or gelatine to give the stock substance. Stock freezes successfully, but flavor and texture are lost after a long time in the freezer.

TROUBLESHOOTING

Removing fat from stock
Chill the stock so the fat solidifies and collects at the top. It can be skimmed from the surface with a spoon. Alternatively, you can remove the fat by dabbing it with paper towels when hot.

MASTER RECIPE

I PREFER A ROBUST STOCK, but for a more delicate flavor, reduce the quantity of vegetables. Experiment by varying them: try pumpkin, zucchini, tomatoes, and even a small quantity of beets, as well as other herbs and spices. For an Asian stock, include a few garlic cloves and a different bouquet garni made with 2 halved stalks lemongrass, 1 inch (2.5cm) piece ginger, sliced into strips, and 1–2 strips orange peel. Substitute 4 star anise and ½ teaspoon Szechwan pepper for the cloves and black peppercorns.

Makes 4–5 cups (1–1.25 liters)

3–4lb (1.5–2kg) chicken bones, or a whole stewing hen, cut into pieces

8 cups (2 liters) water

1 leek, sliced

1 onion, unpeeled, washed well and cut into quarters

4 carrots, chopped

2 celery sticks, chopped

1¼ cups (100g) mushrooms, or 1 tsp dried wild mushrooms such as porcini (optional)

a bouquet garni made with 3 sprigs of thyme, a few celery leaves, 1 bay leaf, and 2–3 strips of lemon peel (see page 30)

4 cloves and 1 tsp black peppercorns tied in a cheesecloth square (optional)

Shelf life: 1 week in the refrigerator; 3 months in the freezer

1 Wash the bones or chicken pieces thoroughly under running water; then drain well. Place in a large stock pot with the water and bring slowly to a boil. Skim any residue that collects on the surface.

2 Simmer for about 30 minutes, skimming when necessary. Add the vegetables, the bouquet garni, and the spice bag.

3 Continue simmering over very low heat, uncovered, for about 1½–2 hours or until the stock has reduced by about a quarter.

4 Cool the stock a little; then strain through a cheesecloth-lined colander; chill quickly and remove the fat (see above).

BROWN STOCK

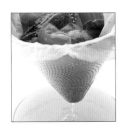

MADE WITH CARE and the freshest ingredients, a good brown stock is crystal clear, deep amber in color, free of fat, and robustly flavored with a balance of vegetables and meat. Experimenting with different vegetables and herbs will subtly alter the flavor of the stock. It is the most time-consuming of the stocks and takes over three hours to prepare, which is why it is prepared less frequently in home kitchens these days. It is still prepared in good restaurants, however, and is an essential ingredient in demi-glazes (see page 60). Traditionally made only from veal bones, it is now made from beef, lamb, or mutton bones.

(see page 60)

TROUBLESHOOTING

Clarifying a cloudy stock
Beat 1–2 egg whites with their shells and add to the stock. Bring to a boil, beating well. Boil for 3 minutes, remove from the heat, and let stand for 10 minutes. Skim off the residue and strain through cheesecloth.

MASTER RECIPE

ROASTING THE BONES for this stock beforehand imparts a mellow yet full and concentrated flavor and gives a rich, deep color. Because the flavors intensify as the stock reduces, it should be seasoned only at the very end of the cooking process.

Makes 4–5 cups (1–1.25 liters)

3lb (1.5kg) beef, lamb, or mutton bones (marrow and ribs), chopped and washed well in a few changes of water

1 calf's foot, halved and cut into quarters (optional)

3 tbsp peanut or light olive oil

1 cup (250ml) dry white wine

12 cups (3 liters) water

1¼ cups (250g) carrots, chopped

2 medium onions, unpeeled, washed well, and cut into quarters

2 celery sticks, chopped

2 garlic cloves, peeled

2 cups (150g) mushrooms, sliced

4 very ripe tomatoes, quartered

a bouquet garni made with 4 sprigs of thyme, 2 celery leaves, and 2 sprigs of parsley (see page 30)

salt and freshly ground black pepper

Shelf life: 1 week in the refrigerator; 3 months in the freezer

(see page 30)

1 *Place the bones and the calf's foot, if using, in a roasting pan and drizzle with the oil. Brown in an oven preheated to 425°F/220°C for 45–50 minutes, turning the bones from time to time. Transfer the bones to a large pan.*

2 *Pour off the fat from the roasting pan. Over low heat, add the wine, stirring and scraping the bottom of the pan. Pour into the pan with the bones; add the water and bring to a boil. Reduce the heat and simmer for 10 minutes.*

3 *Skim any residue from the surface; then add the remaining ingredients, except the salt and pepper. Simmer, uncovered, for about 3 hours.*

4 *Taste and season the stock. Allow to cool a little; then strain through a cheesecloth-lined strainer and cool as quickly as possible.*

FISH STOCK (FUMET)

FISH STOCK, OR FUMET, IS THE BASE for many sauces and soups. Traditionally only the bones and heads of lean white fish such as sole, turbot, or whiting are used, but salmon, trout, and bass also make a good stock. Avoid fatty fish because their strong flavors overpower the stock. Usually white wine is used, but some recipes require red wine. For variety, try replacing the bouquet garni with aromatics such as fennel, dill, ginger, lemongrass, fennel seeds, and caraway.

MASTER RECIPE

FOR A MORE INTENSELY FLAVORED STOCK, add 1 small red mullet. For a delicate flavor, use only fish bones and no heads or trimmings. Do not simmer the stock for longer than 30 minutes as this will give it a bitter flavor.

Makes 5–6 cups (1.25–1.5 liters)

3lb (1.5kg) fish bones, heads, and trimmings

2 tbsp (30g) unsalted butter

2 leeks, white parts only, finely sliced

1 carrot, chopped

1 celery stick, chopped

1 cup (250ml) dry white or red wine

2½ quarts (2.5 liters) water

a bouquet garni made with 2 sprigs of thyme, 2 pieces of green leek leaves, 2 sprigs of parsley, 1 celery leaf, and 1 bay leaf (see below)

10 peppercorns

2–3 thick slices of lemon

Shelf life: 1 week in the refrigerator; 3 months in the freezer

BOUQUET GARNI

To make a bouquet garni, tie a bundle of fresh herbs together with string. It's an ideal way of enhancing the flavor of your stock.

1 Wash the bones thoroughly in plenty of cold water. Drain well.

2 In a pan heat the butter over low heat and sweat the leeks, carrot, and celery until soft.

3 Add the fish bones, the wine, and the water and bring to a boil. Skim off any residue; then add the bouquet garni, peppercorns, and lemon slices and bring back to a boil.

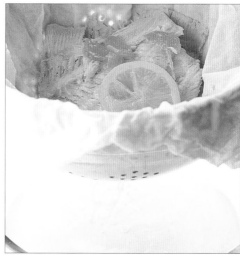

4 Reduce the heat and simmer very gently, uncovered, for 30 minutes, skimming the surface frequently. Strain through a cheesecloth-lined colander and cool as quickly as possible.

VEGETABLE STOCK

I MAKE THIS VERY VERSATILE STOCK using a variety of vegetables and herbs, generally choosing whatever is in season. Choose flavorsome vegetables such as pumpkin, celery root, fennel, parsley, parsnips, or mushrooms but use them sparingly in order not to overwhelm the stock with any one flavor. Include an apple, a pear, or even a peach to add a little sweetness. Use this very versatile stock as a base for sauces, soups, and stews and to make pilafs and risottos.

MASTER RECIPE

EXPERIMENT BY SUBSTITUTING SPICES such as lemongrass, ginger, and star anise for the bouquet garni but choose with the final dish in which you plan to use the stock in mind. Adding ½ cup (75g) sliced okra to the stock will thicken it, giving a slightly gelatinous texture. You can also add 2 tablespoons of either soaked barley, oats, or ground rice to thicken the stock and give it a velvety smoothness.

Makes 1¼ quarts (1–1.25 liters)

1 large onion, sliced into rings

½ cup (100g) carrots, chopped

½ cup (100g) pumpkin, chopped

2 celery sticks

1 large ripe tomato, cut into quarters

3 garlic cloves

1½ quarts (1.5 liters) water

a bouquet garni made with 4 sprigs of parsley, 4 sprigs of cilantro, 2 sprigs of thyme, and 2 strips of lemon peel (see opposite)

Shelf life: 1 week in the refrigerator; 3 months in the freezer

1 Put the chopped onion, carrots, pumpkin, and celery, the quartered tomato, and the garlic in a large pot and add the water.

2 Add the bouquet garni and bring to a boil. Reduce the heat and simmer, uncovered, for 25 minutes. Skim any residue from the surface if necessary.

3 Set the stock aside to cool a little; then strain through a fine mesh strainer into a bowl. Cool the stock as quickly as possible.

BÉCHAMEL SAUCE

A VERSATILE BASE FOR MANY OTHER SAUCES, béchamel is used to add moisture, to bind, and to enrich. It is made with a roux, which is a smooth, cooked mixture of flour and butter that binds and thickens; it is also used in veloutés and some brown sauces. It is important to cook béchamel for 15 minutes so that the flour loses its raw taste and to stir continuously to give a smooth and glossy consistency. Traditionally béchamel sauce is flavored with white pepper, but if, like me, you find black pepper flecks an interesting feature, use it instead because it is much more aromatic. When using béchamel as a binding agent or as a base for baked dishes, simply use milk, but for more delicate pouring sauces infuse the milk to bring out even more flavor in the sauce.

TROUBLESHOOTING

Correcting lumpy béchamel
If you have cooked the sauce too quickly, or not whisked it enough, lumps may form. Lumps can also form if you don't stir the sauce enough and it sticks to the bottom of the pan. Either pass it through a fine strainer or process in a blender or food processor. Return to a clean pan and continue cooking.

MASTER RECIPE

BÉCHAMEL IS MADE with a white roux, which is cooked for about 4 minutes. To make a golden roux for use in veloutés, cook the roux in step 1 for 5–6 minutes, stirring or beating continuously, until it is a golden brown. To make a brown roux, which is sometimes used to thicken brown sauces, use clarified butter (see page 35) and cook over medium heat, stirring or beating continuously, for about 8–10 minutes, until it is a rich brown color.

Makes 1¼ cups (300ml)

For the roux

2 tbsp (30g) butter

¼ cup (30g) flour

For the sauce

2 cups (500ml) milk or
infused milk (see opposite)

freshly grated nutmeg to taste (optional)

salt and freshly ground white or black pepper

Shelf life: 1 week in the refrigerator

1 Melt the butter in a small pan and when it starts to foam, stir in the flour with a wooden spoon until well combined. Cook the roux over a medium heat for 3–4 minutes, stirring continuously; do not allow it to brown.

2 *Add the milk, whisking continuously to
prevent lumps from forming. Bring to a
boil; then reduce the heat and simmer, still
stirring, until the sauce is smooth, about
15–20 minutes.*

3 *Whisk in the nutmeg, if using, and season
with salt and pepper to taste.*

HOLLANDAISE

THIS LIGHT, RICH, AND VERSATILE SAUCE is a glorious invention of the French kitchen although it may, in fact, have been created by French exiles to Holland, hence the name. It is the classic butter emulsion and resembles a warm mayonnaise but is made with clarified butter instead of oil. Deliciously light, Hollandaise is great served with boiled or steamed vegetables, or poached fish. It is also the basis for Béarnaise Sauce (see page 54), which classically accompanies steak. After mastering the technique, experiment with adding different herbs, purées, and spices to create new and exciting versions of this magnificent sauce. Hollandaise should be served warm, never hot. Keep it warm in a bain marie or in a bowl set over a pan of hot water (but keep the water just warmer than lukewarm and do not allow the bottom of the bowl to come into contact with it).

MASTER RECIPE

THIS RICH AND SUBTLE SAUCE goes well with poached fish or steamed vegetables and is a base for many other sauces. Cold Hollandaise makes a very good sandwich spread.

For a slightly richer Mousseline Sauce, fold in ¼ cup (60ml) whipping cream, whipped into soft peaks, just before serving. For a deliciously nutty version of Hollandaise, make noisette butter by gently heating ¼ cup (60g) unsalted butter until it turns a light, nutty brown, and stirring it into the Hollandaise just before serving.

Makes 3 cups (750ml)

4 tbsp water

1 tbsp white wine vinegar

1 tsp white or black peppercorns, crushed

4 egg yolks

1 cup (250g) unsalted butter, clarified (see opposite), cooled to room temperature

1 tbsp lemon juice

salt

1 Put the water, vinegar, and peppercorns into a small pan and simmer over a low heat until reduced by a third, about 2–3 minutes. Pour the reduction through a strainer into a glass or stainless steel bowl; then allow to cool.

2 Place the bowl over a pan of just-simmering water; add the egg yolks and stir until the mixture has thickened and is smooth, about 5–8 minutes. Keep the heat low and do not allow the sauce to get hotter than lukewarm or the eggs might coagulate (see above).

CLARIFYING BUTTER

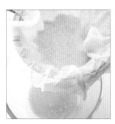

Melt the butter in a small pan over a very low heat; then let it foam up for a few seconds. Skim the foam from the surface and then set the butter aside to cool slightly. Strain the cooled butter through a cheesecloth-lined strainer, leaving the milky sediment behind in the bottom of the pan. Rinsing the cheesecloth in cold water and then wringing it out before using helps to catch any remaining froth.

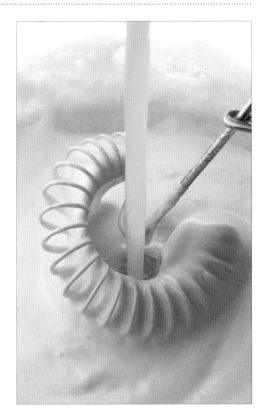

3 Slowly pour in the cooled, clarified butter, stirring continuously until the sauce is thick and fluffy. Mix in the lemon juice and the salt.

4 Smooth, thick, and creamy, the Hollandaise should now hold the trail of the stirring tool. Serve immediately.

SABAYON

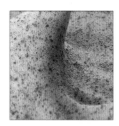

A CLOSE RELATIVE TO ITALIAN ZABAGLIONE (see page 128), sabayon is usually served as a sweet sauce. Instead of the classic sweet wine and sugar, this savory version uses stock, vermouth, and herbs beaten together with egg yolks over a gentle heat to produce a light and airy sauce.

The resulting sabayon is frothy in texture and surprisingly low in fat. Like other sauces containing egg, sabayon should be heated gently and never allowed to near the boiling point to prevent the eggs from coagulating. Sabayon is a marvelous sauce – it never fails to impress and yet, once mastered, you will find that it is quick and not at all difficult to prepare. Sabayon should be served immediately, while it is still warm. See pages 56–57 for further recipes.

TROUBLESHOOTING

What can go wrong
Sabayon is quick and easy to make but if you whisk it for too long, you risk overworking it, which will result in a dense and heavy texture. If you cook it over heat that is too high, or allow the bottom of the bowl to come in contact with the simmering water in the pan, it may separate and the eggs may coagulate. Unfortunately, little can be done to retrieve it; start again.

MASTER RECIPE

THIS IS A DELICATE, HERB-FLECKED SABAYON delicious with poached fish and shellfish. For a sabayon to serve with broiled chicken or other poultry, follow the recipe below but replace the fish stock with ⅔ cup (150ml) chicken stock that has been boiled and reduced down to about ¼ cup (60ml). Substitute 3 tbsp (45ml) white wine for the vermouth, and orange juice for the lemon juice.

Serves 4–6

4 egg yolks

1 tsp sugar

3 tbsp (45ml) Fish Stock (see page 30)

2 tbsp (30ml) dry vermouth

3 tbsp Herb Purée (see page 42)

1 tbsp lemon juice

salt and freshly ground black pepper

1 Place the egg yolks in a large bowl; add the sugar and beat, either by hand or with an electric mixer, until the mixture is well blended and has turned a pale lemon color.

2 Add the fish stock, the dry vermouth, and the herb purée, and continue to beat until they are well blended.

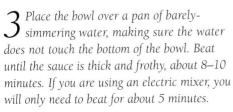 *Place the bowl over a pan of barely-simmering water, making sure the water does not touch the bottom of the bowl. Beat until the sauce is thick and frothy, about 8–10 minutes. If you are using an electric mixer, you will only need to beat for about 5 minutes.*

4 *The sabayon is ready when it is thick enough to leave a ribbon trail on the surface when the beater is lifted from the bowl. Finish by stirring in the lemon juice; then season to taste and serve immediately.*

MAYONNAISE

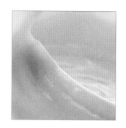

MAKING MAYONNAISE IS A MAGICAL PROCESS: egg yolks, oil, and seasoning are transformed into a rich, glossy emulsion that can be flavored in a multitude of ways. A favorite of cold buffets, mayonnaise can be used as a salad dressing, a dip, an accompaniment to cold meats or seafood, or as a delicious spread for sandwiches and canapés. The secret of success is to make sure all the ingredients are at cool room temperature before you begin. The optional boiling water added at the end extends the storage life of the mayonnnaise and acts as a binding agent, correcting the consistency, if necessary. Making mayonnaise by hand requires plenty of elbow grease, but by using an electric mixer or food processor (see opposite), you can achieve nearly as impressive results in a fraction of the time.

MASTER RECIPE

FOR A STRONGER OLIVE OIL FLAVOR, substitute extra-virgin olive oil for one third of the oil. For a nutty-flavored mayonnaise, replace half the oil with either hazelnut or walnut oil.

Makes 1¼ cups (300ml)

2 egg yolks, at cool room temperature

2 tsp lemon juice or white wine vinegar, plus a little extra to taste

1 tsp Dijon mustard or dry mustard

a small pinch of salt

1¼ cups (300ml) peanut or light olive oil

2 tbsp boiling water (optional)

salt and freshly ground pepper

Shelf life: 1 week in the refrigerator

TROUBLESHOOTING

Correcting curdled mayonnaise
Place 2 tablespoons of the curdled mayonnaise in a clean bowl and add either 2 teaspoons of prepared mustard or an egg yolk and beat until well blended. Beat in the rest of the curdled mayonnaise a little at a time, until thick and glossy. Beat in the boiling water, if using, and the extra lemon juice or vinegar and seasoning.

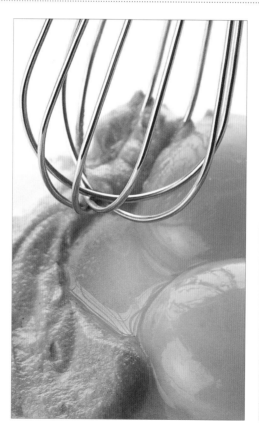

1 Place a mat or dish towel under a mixing bowl to prevent it from slipping. Put the egg yolks, lemon juice or vinegar, mustard, and salt in the bowl and beat together with a balloon whisk until well blended.

2 Start adding the oil one drop at a time, beating continuously, until about one third of it has been incorporated and the mayonnaise is beginning to thicken. It is important not to add the oil too quickly at this stage, or the mayonnaise will curdle (see above).

MACHINE METHODS

Using an Electric Whisk

Beat the egg yolks, lemon juice or vinegar,
mustard, and salt on high speed for
a few seconds. Reduce the speed to
medium and add the oil a little at a time
until one-third has been incorporated.
Add the rest of the oil in a thin, steady
stream until the mayonnaise is thick and
glossy; then increase the mixer to full
speed and finish as in step 3.

Using a Food Processor or Blender

Process the egg yolks, lemon juice or
vinegar, mustard, and salt for a few
seconds. With the machine running, add
the oil in a thin, steady stream until the
mayonnaise is thick and glossy. Finish as
in step 3, but process for only 1–2 seconds
to incorporate the extra ingredients.

*4 Cream-colored and glossy, the
mayonnaise is rich and thick in
consistency and forms stiff peaks.*

*3 Pour in the rest of the oil in a thin, steady
stream, beating constantly, until the
mayonnaise is thick and glossy and forms stiff
peaks. Beat in the extra lemon juice or vinegar
and seasoning to taste. If the mayonnaise is
to be kept, beat in the boiling water.*

CRÈME ANGLAISE

THE CLASSIC AND VERSATILE dessert sauce, crème anglaise, or custard, can be served hot or chilled. Delicious poured over fruit or hot and cold puddings, it is also essential for trifle. Set with gelatine it is a base for bavarois; mixed with fruit and other flavorings, then frozen and churned, it is the basis for ice cream. Try flavoring custard with ingredients ranging from cinnamon sticks and bitter almonds to orange peel, lavender, spirits, and liqueurs. See page 126 for further recipes.

See page 126 for further recipes.

TROUBLESHOOTING

Correcting curdled custard

If the custard has been overcooked or allowed to boil, it will curdle. Pour it through a strainer or process in a blender; then return to a clean pan. Add 2 teaspoons arrowroot or cornstarch slaked with 2 tablespoons milk (see page 44). Cook over gentle heat, whisking constantly and not allowing it to boil, for 1–2 minutes or until thick enough to coat the back of a spoon.

MASTER RECIPE

CUSTARD CAN BE MADE directly on the heat, but this requires practice since it should never be allowed to get hotter than 175°F/80°C. A bowl set over a pan of barely-simmering water or a double boiler are surer ways of controlling heat levels and preventing the custard from curdling. To cool custard, pour into a clean bowl set in a bowl of ice. Stir from time to time to prevent a skin forming. Lay plastic wrap directly on the surface and refrigerate.

Makes 1¼ cups (300ml)

1 vanilla bean, sliced in half lengthwise
or 1 tsp natural vanilla extract

2 cups (500ml) milk

6 egg yolks

3–4 tbsp sugar, or to taste

Shelf life: 1 week in the refrigerator

PREPARING A VANILLA BEAN

Slice the bean in half lengthwise by holding one end and running a sharp knife down the length of it. Scrape the seeds out of the sliced bean.

1 Scrape the vanilla bean (see left) and add the seeds and the bean or the extract to the milk in a pan. Stirring, bring slowly to a boil; then reduce the heat and simmer for 5 minutes.

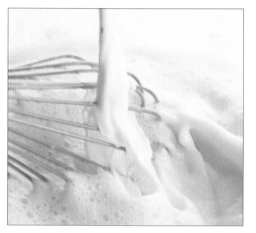

2 In a bowl, beat the egg yolks and sugar until the mixture has lightened and become foamy. Slowly pour the hot milk into the egg mixture while stirring continuously.

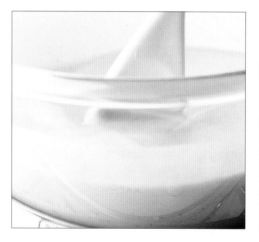

3 Place the bowl over a pan of just-simmering water, making sure the bottom does not touch the water, or pour the mixture, along with the vanilla bean, into the top of a double boiler.

4 Stir continuously until the sauce is thick enough to coat the back of a spoon, about 10–15 minutes. Do not allow the custard to boil. Remove the vanilla bean, if using, and stir well.

CARAMEL

GOLDEN AND CRYSTAL CLEAR, caramel is simply sugar syrup (see page 128) that has been boiled until all the water has evaporated. When it reaches 309°F/154°C it starts to caramelize and gives off a pleasant aroma. Use caramel hot to line moulds for *crème caramel* or make spun sugar by pouring it on a lightly greased spoon to set. Left to set and then broken up, caramel makes a crunchy topping and can also be used in a powder form to add instant flavor to sweet sauces and custards (see right).

(see page 128)

CARAMEL CRUNCH

To make caramel crunch or powder, crush the broken shards in a mortar and pestle until fine.

MASTER RECIPE

THE LAST STAGE in the cooking process is crucial and happens very quickly so be on guard: watch constantly. In no time at all caramel can start smoking and then burn – at which point it is irretrievable. To stop the caramel from cooking further, plunge the bottom of the pan into cold water the moment the right color is achieved.

Makes 1¼ cups (300ml) liquid caramel, ½lb (250g) caramel crunch

1 cup + 2 tbsp (250g) sugar

5 tbsp water

Shelf life: up to 1 year as broken pieces or a crushed powder, stored in a tightly sealed jar

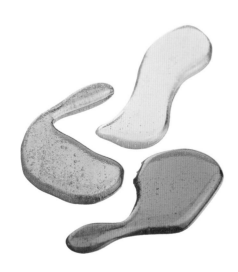

1 Place the sugar and water in a pan and heat gently, shaking the pan, until all the sugar has dissolved. Bring slowly to a boil; the syrup will begin to caramelize.

2 It turns from pale gold to light brown and finally to dark brown. Remove from the heat and plunge the bottom of the pan into cold water as soon as the right color is achieved.

3 When the caramel reaches the desired color and consistency, it is ready for use in its liquid form or can be carefully poured onto a lightly oiled surface to harden.

4 Allow the caramel to cool and become hard; then crack it with a pestle, wooden mallet or rolling pin. The broken caramel pieces make a delicious and elegant cake decoration.

HERB PURÉE

THIS IS AN EASY WAY OF ADDING INSTANT COLOR and flavor to sauces and dips. Fresh herbs are briefly blanched then puréed, which captures their flavor and extends their storage life. The purée can be refrigerated or frozen (use ice cube trays, see pages 134–35). Tender, mild herbs such as flat-leaf parsley, basil, dill, cilantro, and sorrel – or a mixture of them all – work best. Strong-flavored herbs with tough leaves, such as thyme, sage, and rosemary, tend to be bitter and difficult to purée.

MASTER RECIPE

THIS IS THE QUICKEST and most convenient way that I know of storing fresh herbs. Remember to blanch the herbs only briefly, otherwise their flavors will be destroyed. To achieve a smooth paste, spend time removing any tough stems or leaves; use young, bright green leaves and discard any that are either wilted or discolored.

Makes ½ cup (100g)

4 cups (1 liter) water

2 tsp sugar

1 cup (150g) fresh herbs, leaves only

olive oil to drizzle

Shelf life: 1 week in the refrigerator; 3 months in the freezer

1 Bring the water to a rapid boil and stir in the sugar. Add the herbs and bring back to a boil; then immediately remove from the heat and fish out the herbs with a skimmer or slotted spoon.

2 Plunge the blanched leaves into a large bowl of ice water. Swirl the wilted leaves around, then drain. Squeeze out all the remaining water with your hands.

3 Put the blanched herbs into a food processor with 1–2 tablespoons of water and process into a fine purée, or chop to a smooth purée by hand using a mezzaluna or hachoir.

4 Rinse a large piece of cheesecloth in cold water, wring well, then use, doubled, to line a strainer. Place over a bowl; pour in the herb purée and drain in a cool place for 2 hours.

5 Discard any liquid that has collected in the bowl and scrape the purée into a small dish. Pour a thin layer of olive oil over the purée, cover, and refrigerate.

TOMATO PASTE

THIS FRESH TOMATO PASTE is a far superior alternative to store-bought tomato paste. I use it to add a delicate pink tint and a remarkably fragrant tomato flavor to many dishes; it is also very useful for thickening sauces, soup, and stews. It is important to use firm-fleshed, solid tomatoes, such as Italian plum or beefsteak tomatoes, and, where possible, to choose vine-ripened varieties because they are brightly colored and provide the best flavor.

MASTER RECIPE

I MAKE THIS IN LARGE QUANTITIES whenever ripe, flavorful tomatoes are available. Save the surprisingly clear juice that drains from the tomatoes – it is full of flavor and makes a delicious base for soups.

Makes ½ cup (100g)

2lb (1kg) fragrant cooking tomatoes, peeled (see below), seeded, and coarsely chopped

3 tbsp lemon juice

olive oil to drizzle

Shelf life: 1 week in the refrigerator; 3 months in the freezer

1 Put the tomatoes and lemon juice in a food processor and process until a smooth paste is achieved. Rinse a large piece of cheesecloth in cold water, wring well, and use, doubled, to line a colander or strainer.

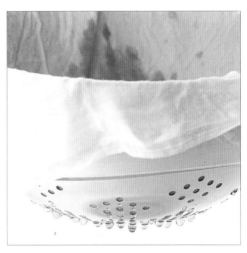

2 Place the cheesecloth-lined colander or strainer over a deep bowl; then pour in the processed tomatoes. Cover with plastic wrap; then allow to drain in the refrigerator for about 2 hours.

PEELING TOMATOES

With a sharp knife, cut out the core, then make a slit down the side of each tomato. Put the tomatoes in a bowl, pour over boiling water to cover and let them stand for a couple of minutes. The hot water loosens the skin and it can then be easily peeled away with a sharp knife.

To seed, simply cut the tomato into quarters and scrape away the seeds.

3 Pour out the clear tomato juice that has collected in the bottom of the bowl (or reserve it for another use). Scrape the paste into a small dish.

4 Pour a thin layer of olive oil over the paste, cover, and refrigerate.

THICKENING SAUCES

MODERN COOKS TEND TO SERVE LIGHTER, THINNER SAUCES and to avoid using heavy starches. Yet there are always variables when cooking, and from time to time a thickener is needed to achieve the right consistency. The most common technique for thickening is through reduction – rapid boiling until a glossy, syrupy consistency is reached. Sauces can also be thickened with the addition of starch such as cornstarch or arrowroot, which expands when added to a boiling liquid and absorbs the liquid to give a permanent, thickened suspension. Although each technique gives a slightly different finish to a sauce, many are interchangeable; consult Troubleshooting on pages 136–37 for specific advice.

THICKENING WITH CORNSTARCH

THIS GIVES A SHINY, light, and opaque finish to almost any sauce. Usually 2–3 teaspoons of cornstarch are enough for about 2 cups (500ml) liquid; mix equal quantities of cornstarch and a cool liquid such as water, stock, or wine – a process known as slaking. Add the mixture to the sauce a little at a time and boil briefly until the right consistency is achieved.

1 Mix the cornstarch and liquid until a smooth paste of pouring consistency is achieved.

2 Pour the mixture into boiling sauce and boil for 1 minute, beating or stirring continuously.

3 The thickened sauce will coat the back of a spoon. The sauce will not thin if reheated or boiled.

THICKENING WITH ARROWROOT

ONE OF THE MOST VERSATILE thickeners, arrowroot produces a clear, light sauce that can also be used as a glaze. Add about 2–3 teaspoons of arrowroot for 2 cups (500ml) liquid, although you may need to add a little more if the liquid is acidic. As with cornstarch, use equal quantities of arrowroot and a cool liquid such as water, stock, or wine.

1 Mix the arrowroot and liquid until a smooth, pourable paste is achieved.

2 Pour the mixture into boiling sauce and boil, beating or stirring, for no longer than a minute.

3 The sauce thickens immediately and becomes glossy; it evenly coats the back of a spoon.

THICKENING BY REDUCTION

THIS TECHNIQUE gives an intensely flavored, aromatic sauce that is best served in small quantities. Use this method of thickening for demi-glazes, gravies, and stock-based sauces. Skimming the sauce from time to time while it reduces can prevent the sauce from becoming cloudy.

1 Boil the sauce over a medium heat; as it reduces and the water evaporates, it should thicken.

2 The sauce will continue to thicken for as long as you continue to boil it.

THICKENING WITH BUTTER

THE PROCESS OF ADDING butter to a sauce to thicken it is known as mounting (from the French *monter*); it produces a creamy, glossy sauce that thinly coats the back of a spoon. Always use fresh, well-chilled unsalted butter and be sure to add it a little at a time. Finish the sauce with a few drops of lemon juice and serve immediately.

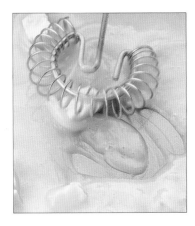

1 Bring the sauce to the boil, then, off the heat, whisk in chilled cubes of unsalted butter.

2 Add the butter gradually until the sauce is rich and glossy and coats the back of a spoon.

THICKENING WITH BEURRE MANIÉ (KNEADED BUTTER)

IDEAL FOR THICKENING and adding gloss to soups, stews, and gravies, beurre manié is the kitchen's most valuable fixer. It should be added in small quantities until the right consistency is achieved. Use only unsalted butter to make beurre manié. It can be prepared in advance and frozen.

1 With a palette knife, mash equal quantities of all-purpose flour and softened butter into a smooth paste.

2 Gradually add the paste to boiling sauce, stirring or beating until it has dispersed.

3 Boil for 2–3 minutes to cook the flour. The sauce should thicken enough to coat the spoon.

RECIPES

FROM CLASSICS SUCH AS HOLLANDAISE AND

BÉCHAMEL TO SIMPLE DRESSINGS AND

SALSAS, THE FOLLOWING PAGES CELEBRATE

SAUCES IN THE BROADEST SENSE OF THE

WORD. A MEDLEY OF RECIPES IS OFFERED;

SOME ARE OLD FAVORITES WHILE OTHERS

HAVE BEEN SPECIALLY CREATED FOR THIS

BOOK. LOOK FOR NOVEL AND IMAGINATIVE

WAYS TO SERVE THESE VERSATILE SAUCES.

CLASSIC SAUCES

IT IS DIFFICULT TO DEFINE CLASSIC SAUCES – WHAT IS CLASSIC TO ONE PALATE IS COMPLETELY ALIEN TO

ANOTHER. THESE CLASSIC SAUCES ARE MOSTLY FRENCH IN ORIGIN, BUT MANY ARE REPRESENTATIVE OF NEW

TRENDS IN CONTEMPORARY CUISINE AND INTRODUCE EXOTIC INGREDIENTS THAT ARE MORE READILY AVAILABLE.

HERE IS AN EXCITING AND DIVERSE COLLECTION OF FLAVORSOME SAUCES TO SUIT TODAY'S LIFESTYLE.

WHITE SAUCES

BÉCHAMEL-BASED SAUCES are quick and straightforward to make as well as being incredibly versatile. A cheese version is wonderful on pasta; others can be poured over fish, eggs, or vegetables and lightly broiled until golden.

Béchamel-based sauces will last for up to a week in the refrigerator. They should be reheated gently; you may need to add a little milk to improve the consistency. The master recipe for Béchamel is on pages 32–33.

SOUBISE

Named after a French army commander, this smooth and satisfying sauce is especially good with lamb, roasted poultry, and game birds. Traditionally the sauce is strained, but for a more intense onion flavor, simply process in a blender or food processor until smooth.

Advance preparation: the béchamel can be made in advance

Shelf life: 3 days in the refrigerator (brush the top with butter to prevent a skin from forming); 3 months in the freezer

3 tbsp (50g) butter

1¼ cups (300g) onions, finely chopped

1 recipe Béchamel Sauce (see pages 32–33)

3 tbsp heavy cream

freshly grated nutmeg to taste

lemon juice to taste (optional)

salt and freshly ground white or black pepper

1 Melt the butter in a small pan; add the onions, then sauté until soft and translucent, about 10–15 minutes.

2 Meanwhile, in a separate pan, heat the béchamel to the boiling point. Add it to the onions and slowly bring to a boil, stirring continuously. Reduce the heat as soon as it reaches boiling point and simmer, stirring frequently, for 30 minutes, or until the onions are very tender.

3 Process the sauce in a food processor or blender, or pour it through a strainer into a clean pan, pressing through as much of the onion as possible. Add the cream.

4 Bring to a boil; reduce the heat and simmer, stirring constantly, for about 5–8 minutes, until it is very thick. Season to taste with the nutmeg, lemon juice, if using, and salt and pepper.

VARIATION

CARAMELIZED SOUBISE
Serve this modern take on Soubise with vegetables and game birds. Follow the recipe above, but use only 2 tablespoons (30g) butter and add 2 tablespoons olive oil. Increase the amount of onion to 1lb (500g). When the onions are translucent, increase the heat to medium and add 1 tablespoon dark brown sugar and 2 tablespoons balsamic vinegar. Cook for a further 15–20 minutes until golden and caramelized, then add the hot béchamel and finish as for Soubise. For a thinner consistency, stir in 1–2 tablespoons milk or cream.

MUSHROOM SAUCE

This vegetarian version of Supreme Sauce (see page 53) goes as well with cooked vegetables as it does with roast chicken. The sauce can be served smooth, but I prefer to leave in the mushrooms.

Advance preparation: the béchamel can be made in advance

Shelf life: 3 days in the refrigerator (brush the top with butter to prevent a skin from forming); 3 months in the freezer

1 recipe Béchamel Sauce (see pages 32–33)
1½ cups (100g) button mushrooms, thinly sliced
1 tbsp lemon juice
grated lemon peel to taste
¼ tsp sweet paprika
cayenne pepper to taste
2 tbsp (30g) butter, chilled and cut into pieces
salt

1 Bring the béchamel to a boil; add the mushrooms and simmer over very low heat for about 10 minutes. Stir the sauce continuously to prevent it sticking to the bottom of the pan.

2 Remove from the heat and either leave the mushrooms in the sauce or pour the sauce through a strainer to remove them.

3 Add the lemon juice, grated peel, and paprika; then add cayenne pepper and salt to taste. Beat in the butter a few pieces at a time until melted, then serve.

ROBUST MUSHROOM SAUCE

¼ cup (50g) butter
1½ cups (100g) cremini mushrooms, chopped
¼ cup (15g) dried porcini mushrooms, soaked in ¼ cup (60ml) hot water for 30 minutes
1 recipe Béchamel Sauce (see pages 32–33)
1 tbsp soy sauce
1 tbsp lemon juice
¼ tsp grated lemon peel
1–2 tbsp chopped fresh chervil or parsley
salt and freshly ground black pepper

1 Heat the butter in a small pan; add the fresh mushrooms and sauté until softened, about 5 minutes. Drain the porcini, reserving the soaking liquid; chop them finely and add to the pan. Sauté for about 2 minutes, then add the soaking liquid, the béchamel, and the soy sauce. Simmer for 20 minutes.

2 Remove from the heat and stir in the lemon juice and peel. Season to taste and stir in the chervil or parsley.

This is very quick to make and delicious with beef, game birds, and even pasta. If you prefer a smoother consistency, purée the sauce in a blender or food processor, or pour through a strainer before seasoning.

Advance preparation: the béchamel can be made in advance

Shelf life: 3 days in the refrigerator (brush the top with butter to prevent a skin from forming); 3 months in the freezer

MORNAY SAUCE

This classic cheese sauce is traditionally flavored with Emmenthal, Gruyère, or farmhouse Cheddar, but you could experiment with freshly grated Parmesan, Spanish Manchego, or, for an orange cheese sauce, red Leicester. For a lighter version, omit the cream.

Advance preparation: the béchamel can be made in advance

Shelf life: 3 days in the refrigerator (brush the top with butter to prevent a skin from forming); 3 months in the freezer

See page 19 for illustration

1 recipe Béchamel Sauce (see pages 32–33)
⅓ cup (75ml) heavy cream
¾ cup (100g) Emmenthal, Gruyère, or Cheddar, grated
freshly grated nutmeg to taste
freshly ground black pepper

1 Place the béchamel and cream in a small pan and bring to a boil. Lower the heat and simmer gently, whisking continuously to prevent sticking, for about 5 minutes.

2 Add the cheese and whisk for about a minute, or until all of it has melted and the sauce is smooth.

3 Remove from the heat and whisk in nutmeg and pepper to taste.

VARIATION

BLUE CHEESE SAUCE

Follow the recipe for Mornay, using only ¼ cup (60ml) heavy cream, and stiring in ¾ cup (75g) freshly grated Parmesan in place of the Emmenthal, Gruyère, or Cheddar. Stir in ¾ cup (100g) crumbled blue cheese with the nutmeg, plus 4–5 chopped sage leaves and seasoning to taste. Heat for about 1 minute to melt the cheese, then serve.

EXOTIC BÉCHAMEL

An interesting variation of the classic béchamel, this exotic sauce is particularly good with steamed vegetables and broiled fish. The secret of its light texture is the long simmering time. For a smoother sauce, use unbleached white flour. Using coconut milk or soy milk makes a good vegan option.

Shelf life: 1 week in the refrigerator; 3 months in the freezer

2 tbsp peanut or sunflower oil
½ cup (40g) whole wheat flour
2 cups (500ml) coconut milk or Infused Milk (see page 33)
2 tbsp (30g) fresh ginger, chopped
4 tbsp (50g) shallots, finely chopped
1 garlic clove, finely chopped
1 red chili, seeded and finely chopped
1 tbsp lime juice
salt

1 Heat the oil in a pan; add the flour and cook, stirring, until it begins to smell pleasantly nutty, about 5 minutes.

2 Add the milk and bring slowly to a boil, beating continuously to prevent the sauce from sticking to the bottom of the pan.

3 When the sauce has thickened to the consistency of heavy cream, transfer it to a double boiler or a bowl placed over a pan of simmering water. Cover and cook gently for about 45 minutes, stirring frequently to prevent a skin from forming.

4 Add all the remaining ingredients except the lime juice and salt, and cook for a further 15 minutes, stirring frequently. Remove from the heat, stir in the lime juice, add salt to taste, and serve immediately.

AURORA ▷

½ recipe Béchamel (see pages 32–33)
⅓ cup (75ml) heavy cream
½ cup (125g) Cooked Tomato Coulis (see page 59) or Tomato Paste (see page 43)
2 tbsp (30g) butter, chilled and cubed
1 tsp lemon juice
fresh basil leaves, minced (optional)
cayenne pepper to taste
salt and freshly ground black pepper

1 Combine the béchamel and cream in a small pan; bring to a boil and simmer for about 5 minutes.

2 Add the tomato coulis or purée and simmer for 5 minutes, stirring constantly.

3 Remove from the heat and beat in the butter a little at a time. Strain the sauce, add the lemon juice and basil, if using, and the cayenne; season to taste.

A tomato-flavored béchamel that tastes good served with turkey, chicken, or vegetables. If you prefer, use canned tomato paste, but add 1–2 tablespoons of grated onion, 1 minced garlic clove, and a sprig of sage, thyme, or rosemary to boost the flavor.

Advance preparation: the béchamel can be made in advance

Shelf life: 3 days in the refrigerator

PARSLEY SAUCE

1 recipe Béchamel (see pages 32–33)
¼ cup (60ml) heavy cream (optional)
3 tbsp chopped fresh parsley
1 tsp lemon juice
finely grated lemon peel to taste
salt and freshly ground black pepper

1 Bring the béchamel and cream to a boil in a pan, then remove from the heat.

2 Stir in the parsley, lemon juice, and the peel. Season to taste and serve.

Traditionally served with cooked ham, parsley sauce is also good with broiled or steamed fish or chicken.

Advance preparation: the béchamel can be made in advance

Shelf life: 3 days in the refrigerator

VARIATION

MIXED HERB SAUCE
To make an herb sauce, delicious with steamed vegetables or poached chicken, follow the recipe above, but beat in 2–3 tablespoons hazelnut oil instead of the cream. Remove from the heat and stir in 1 tablespoon each of chopped fresh tarragon, thyme, and chervil in place of the parsley.

VELOUTÉ SAUCES

RICH AND VELVETY, VELOUTÉ SAUCE is made from the same roux base as Béchamel (see pages 32–33), but using stock instead of milk makes it thinner and lighter and gives it a smooth texture. The flavor depends on the quality of your stock: homemade is best, but canned stock will do; use bouillon cubes only in emergencies. Use a stock that complements the food you are serving: chicken stock with chicken, for example.

VELOUTÉ

The ideal consistency of a velouté is that of a smooth pouring sauce that thinly coats the back of a spoon. If a thicker consistency is preferred, stir in up to 3 tbsp (50g) beurre manié (see page 45) before straining and simmer for a further 5–8 minutes.

Advance preparation: the stock can be made in advance

Shelf life: 2–3 days in the refrigerator; 1 month in the freezer

1 recipe White or Blonde Roux (see page 32)
3¼ cups (750ml) Stock (see pages 28–31)
strained lemon juice to taste (optional)
salt and freshly ground black pepper

1 Heat the roux in a small pan, then add the stock and bring to a boil, beating continuously with a wire whisk.

2 Reduce the heat to minimum and simmer the velouté for 30 minutes, skimming any residue off the surface and stirring every now and then.

3 Strain the velouté through a sieve, add lemon juice, if desired, and season to taste.

CAPER SAUCE

This traditional British sauce is delicious served with braised lamb but is also surprisingly good with chicken and fish.

Advance preparation: the velouté can be made in advance

Shelf life: 2–3 days in the refrigerator

1 recipe Velouté made with Chicken or Lamb Stock (see above)
3 tbsp capers in brine, drained and chopped
1–2 anchovy fillets, chopped (optional)
1 tbsp lemon juice
a few gratings of lemon peel
2 tbsp chopped fresh parsley, mint, or dill
salt and freshly ground black pepper

1 Bring the velouté to a boil in a pan and add the capers and the anchovies, if using. Reduce the heat and simmer for 10 minutes, stirring frequently to prevent scorching.

2 Season, then add the lemon juice and peel. Stir in the herbs just before serving.

LEMONGRASS & COCONUT SAUCE

3 tbsp (50g) butter
½ cup (100g) shallots, finely chopped
2 lemongrass stalks, hard outer layers removed, finely chopped
1 garlic clove, minced
2 tbsp unbleached flour, sifted
1 cup (250ml) Fish Stock (see page 30)
1 cup (250ml) coconut milk
1 small red chili, chopped
4 kaffir lime leaves, finely shredded
1 tsp light brown sugar (optional)
2 tbsp lime juice
2 tbsp Thai fish sauce (*nam pla*) or salt

A spicy, piquant sauce, very good served with grilled or fried firm-fleshed fish such as barramundi or kingclip. It also goes well with white fish such as cod or halibut.

Advance preparation: the stock can be made in advance

Shelf life: 2–3 days in the refrigerator

1 Heat the butter in a small pan; add the shallots, lemongrass, and garlic and sauté gently, stirring often, until the shallots start to color, about 5 minutes. Sprinkle in the flour and cook, stirring, until the shallots are lightly browned, about 4–5 minutes.

2 Add the fish stock and coconut milk, stirring well to incorporate any bits that have stuck to the bottom of the pan. Bring to a boil, then reduce the heat and simmer gently for about 30 minutes, stirring from time to time to prevent sticking.

3 Pour the sauce through a strainer into a clean pan. Add the chili, kaffir lime leaves, and sugar, if using. Bring to a boil, then reduce the heat and simmer for 2 minutes. Remove from the heat and stir in the lime juice and fish sauce or salt.

SUPREME SAUCE

A classic sauce for chicken, and one of the most delicate. If you prefer more texture, do not strain the sauce.

Advance preparation: the velouté can be made in advance

Shelf life: 2–3 days in the refrigerator

1 recipe Velouté made with Chicken Stock (see opposite)
1 cup (75g) mushrooms, thinly sliced
4 tbsp heavy cream
2 tbsp (30g) butter, chilled and cubed
lemon juice to taste (optional)
4 tbsp dry sherry (optional)
salt and freshly ground black pepper

1 Heat the velouté in a small pan. Stir in the mushrooms and cream. Simmer gently for about 10 minutes, stirring frequently to prevent sticking.

2 Strain the sauce into a clean pan over a medium heat. Beat in the butter, one piece at a time. Remove from the heat, add the lemon juice and sherry, if using; season to taste and serve.

OLIVE OIL SAUCE

A robust and flavorful sauce that is very low in cholesterol since it is made with olive oil instead of butter. It goes well with chicken or broiled fish. You could use canned roasted, peeled peppers instead.

Advance preparation: the stock can be made in advance

Shelf life: 2–3 days in the refrigerator

½ cup (60g) all-purpose flour
4 tbsp extra-virgin olive oil
2 cups (500ml) Chicken Stock (see page 28)
1 large red pepper, roasted, peeled, seeded, and finely chopped (see page 96)
½ cup (75g) green olives, pitted and chopped
1 garlic clove, crushed to a paste with a little salt
2 tbsp chopped fresh flat-leaf parsley (optional)
salt and freshly ground black pepper

1 Make a roux with the flour and 3 tablespoons of the oil (see page 32). Add the stock and bring to a boil, stirring.

2 Reduce the heat and skim the foam from the surface. Add the red pepper and simmer for 30 minutes, stirring frequently.

3 Add the olives and garlic and simmer for 2–3 minutes. Season, beat in the rest of the oil, and stir in the parsley, if using.

MUSTARD SAUCE

⅓ cup (75ml) white wine
⅓ cup (75ml) orange juice
½ tsp grated orange peel
1 tbsp white wine vinegar
½ tsp coriander seeds, crushed
2 tsp dry mustard
1 recipe Velouté, made with Chicken Stock (see opposite)
3 tbsp heavy cream or crème fraîche
2 tbsp grainy mustard
salt and freshly ground black pepper

This light orange and mustard-flavored sauce is delicious with roast or poached poultry or poached salmon.

Advance preparation: the velouté can be made in advance

Shelf life: 2–3 days in the refrigerator

1 Place the wine, orange juice and peel, vinegar, coriander seeds, and dry mustard in a small pan and bring to a rapid boil, mixing well. Boil for 8–10 minutes, until the liquid is reduced to 3 tablespoons. Remove from the heat and strain the reduction into a clean pan.

2 Heat the velouté, then stir it into the strained reduction and bring to a boil. Reduce the heat and simmer for 5 minutes, stirring frequently. Stir in the cream and mustard, then season to taste and serve.

VARIATION

MUSTARD SAUCE FOR FISH
Easily adapted, this sauce makes a delectable accompaniment to poached fish, salmon in particular. Substitute fish stock (see page 30) for the chicken stock and fennel seeds for the coriander seeds.

BUTTER EMULSIONS

THESE SAUCES ARE A DELICATE MIXTURE of butter and egg yolks emulsified by vigorous beating over gentle heat. The sauce created is thick, opaque, and creamy.

The classic butter emulsion is Hollandaise, invented by French Huguenots exiled in Holland. The master recipe can be found on pages 34–35.

BÉARNAISE SAUCE

A more robust version of Hollandaise (see pages 34–35), this sauce is best suited to broiled meats and salmon.

5 tbsp dry white wine
5 tbsp white wine vinegar
2 shallots, finely chopped
4 tbsp chopped fresh tarragon
10 peppercorns, crushed
4 egg yolks
1 cup (250g) unsalted butter, clarified (see page 35) then cooled to room temperature, or the same amount of chilled and cubed butter
1 tbsp chopped fresh chervil (optional)
2 tbsp lemon juice

1 Put the wine, vinegar, shallots, 2 tablespoons of the tarragon, and the peppercorns in a small pan. Simmer until reduced by half. Remove from the heat and allow to cool.

2 Pour the reduction through a strainer into a stainless-steel or glass bowl. Place the bowl over a pan of just-simmering water, making sure that the bottom of the bowl does not touch the water. Add the egg yolks and stir constantly over low heat until the mixture thickens, about 5–8 minutes.

3 If using clarified butter, pour it in slowly, beating continuously, until the sauce is thick and fluffy. If you are using chilled, cubed butter, add a few pieces at a time, beating continuously to blend it in completely. Stir in the remaining tarragon, the chervil, if using, and the lemon juice. Serve immediately.

BEURRE BLANC

3 shallots, finely chopped
3 tbsp white wine vinegar
⅔ cup (150ml) dry white wine or water
1 cup (250g) unsalted butter, chilled and cubed
a few drops of lemon juice
salt and freshly ground black pepper

A rich accompaniment to fish, beurre blanc, or butter sauce, is light, delicious, and extremely rich. It is very easy to make if you remember that, like custard, it should never be allowed to boil. This butter emulsion does not contain egg yolks.

1 Combine the shallots and vinegar in a small pan and bring to a boil. Cook over medium heat until most of the vinegar has evaporated, then add the wine or water and simmer until reduced by half.

2 Over low heat, add the butter one piece at a time, beating continuously to blend it into the sauce between each addition. When all the butter has been blended in, stir in the lemon juice, season with salt and freshly ground black pepper, and serve immediately.

VARIATIONS

ORANGE BUTTER SAUCE
Another favorite with fish; I like to serve this with salmon or cod. Follow the recipe above, but reduce the wine or water to ½ cup (100ml) and add ¼ cup (60ml) orange juice.

LEMONGRASS BUTTER SAUCE *See page 13 for illustration*
My version of a Thai butter sauce, this suits delicately flavored fish such as trout and salmon. Follow the recipe above, but use 11 tablespoons (160g) chilled and cubed butter and 6 tablespoons (90g) chilled and cubed Lemongrass and Lime Butter (see page 74).

CHILI BUTTER SAUCE
Serve this piquant butter sauce with fish, chicken, or vegetables. Follow the recipe above, but use ½ cup (125g) chilled and cubed butter and ½ cup (125g) chilled and cubed Chili Butter (see page 74).

MALTAISE ▷

This is particularly good with poached salmon.

Advance preparation: the reduction (step 1) can be made in advance

½ cup (100ml) blood orange juice or ordinary orange juice

peel of 1 orange, thinly pared and cut into fine julienne

1 recipe Hollandaise (see pages 34–35)

1 In a small pan, simmer the orange juice until it has reduced by a third. In another pan, blanch the orange peel in boiling water for 1 minute, then drain, refresh in cold water, and drain again. Add the blanched peel to the reduced orange juice and simmer gently for 1 minute.

2 Stir the orange juice reduction into the Hollandaise just before serving.

EXOTIC HOLLANDAISE

Sharp, light, and refreshing, this sauce is especially suitable for firm-fleshed fish such as tuna or swordfish.

Advance preparation: the reduction (step 1) can be made in advance

½ cup (100ml) dry white wine or Fish Stock (see page 30)

2 lemongrass stalks, hard outer layers removed, finely chopped

¼ cup (50g) shallots, finely chopped

½ inch (1cm) piece ginger, finely chopped

1 recipe Hollandaise, made without the lemon juice (see pages 34–35)

2 tbsp lime juice

½ tsp grated lime peel

3 kaffir lime leaves, finely shredded (optional)

½ tsp chopped fresh red chili or freshly ground black pepper

salt

1 Put the wine or stock, lemongrass, shallots, and ginger in a small pan and boil until reduced by half. Remove from the heat and allow to cool.

2 Strain the reduction into a stainless steel or glass bowl. Finish as for Béarnaise Sauce (opposite) from step 2 but stir in the lime juice, peel, lime leaves, if using, and chili instead of the herbs and lemon juice. Season with salt and serve.

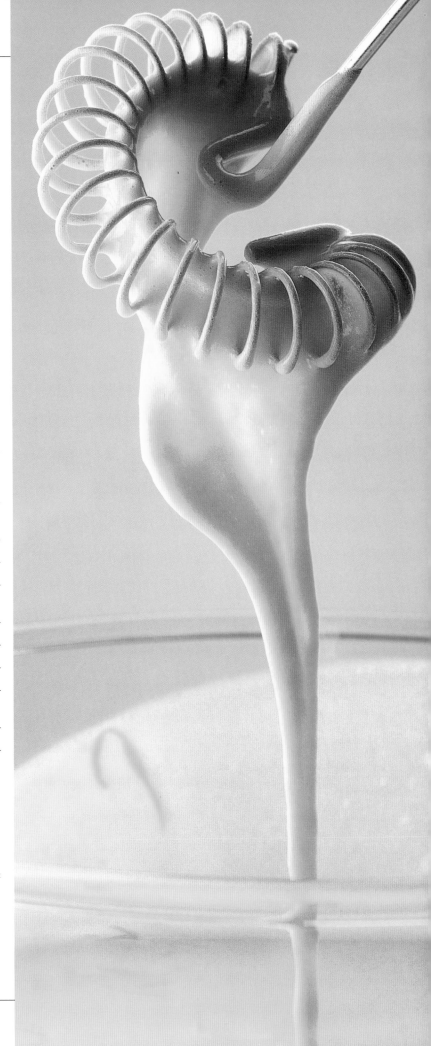

RIGHT: ORANGE JUICE GIVES MALTAISE A DELICATE ORANGE HUE

SABAYONS

LIGHT, FLUFFY, AND DELICATELY FLAVORED, sabayons are easy to make and yet always look impressive. After mastering the technique (see master recipe, pages 36–37), try using different herbs in the reduction. The golden rule to remember is the proportion of ⅓ cup + 2 tablespoons (100ml) liquid to 4 egg yolks. Up to 5 tablespoons (75g) clarified butter (see page 35) can be beaten into it before serving to create a richer – but less fluffy – sabayon.

◁ PINK CHAMPAGNE SABAYON

Perfect as a light and delicately flavored accompaniment to poached shellfish or broiled lobster.

4 egg yolks
2 tbsp champagne vinegar or white wine vinegar
⅓ cup (90ml) pink champagne
salt and freshly ground black pepper

1 Place the egg yolks in a bowl; add the vinegar and beat either by hand or with an electric mixer until the mixture becomes pale yellow. Add the champagne and beat well.

2 Place the bowl over a pan of just-simmering water, making sure the base of the bowl does not touch the water and continue beating for 8–10 minutes, until the sauce is thick and frothy. Season to taste and serve immediately.

VARIATION

SEAFOOD SABAYON

Follow the recipe above but use only 1 tablespoon white wine vinegar and substitute 2 tablespoons Ricard and ½ cup (100ml) Fish Stock (see page 30) for the champagne.

AVGOLEMONO

This classic Greek sauce is slightly sharp in flavor and goes particularly well with poached or roast chicken, or over steamed vegetables.

Advance preparation: the chicken stock can be made in advance

½ cup (125ml) Chicken Stock (see page 28)
2 tsp cornstarch
strained juice of 3 lemons
grated peel of 1 lemon
3 egg yolks, well beaten
salt and freshly ground black pepper

1 Bring the chicken stock to a boil in a small pan. Dissolve the cornstarch in the lemon juice and add to the stock with the lemon peel. Stirring well, bring the sauce back to a boil.

2 Reduce the heat and add the egg yolks in a thin, steady stream, beating continuously. Continue beating for 1–2 minutes until the sauce thickens slightly. Remove from the heat, season to taste, and serve immediately.

ORANGE & SAFFRON SABAYON

strained juice of 2 oranges
1 cup (250ml) Chicken or Fish Stock (see pages 28 and 30)
½ tsp coriander seeds, dry-roasted and crushed (see page 78)
½ tsp saffron threads, soaked in 2 tbsp warmed brandy
4 egg yolks
1 tbsp lemon juice
grated peel of ½ orange
salt and freshly ground black pepper

Elegant, frothy, flavorsome, and brilliantly colored, this sabayon is wonderful served with chicken or fish.

Advance preparation: the reduction (step 1) can be made in advance

1 Put the orange juice, stock, coriander seeds, and dissolved saffron in a small pan and boil rapidly until the mixture is reduced to approximately ⅓ cup (100ml). Remove from the heat and allow to cool.

2 Place the egg yolks in a bowl; add the cooled reduction and the lemon juice and beat, either by hand or with an electric mixer, until the mixture has turned slightly paler.

3 Place the bowl over a pan of just-simmering water, making sure the water does not touch the bottom of the bowl. Beat until the sauce is thick and frothy, about 8–10 minutes. Add the orange peel, season, and serve immediately.

OPPOSITE: PINK CHAMPAGNE SABAYON WITH ASPARAGUS, SCALLOPS, AND SALMON CAVIAR

COULIS

IN FRENCH, THE WORD *COULIS* refers to a thin purée of fish, poultry, or vegetables often used to thicken soups and stews. In modern cooking, it means raw or cooked fruit or vegetable purées that are diluted to a pouring consistency with stock, wine, or, in the case of sweet coulis, sugar syrup. Coulis are wonderful in their simplicity – once you have mastered the technique, experiment with different vegetables, herbs, and fruit.

WATERCRESS COULIS

A delicious accompaniment to fish or cooked vegetables.

Advance preparation: the stock can be made in advance

3 bunches of watercress, leaves and stems separated, stems of 1 bunch chopped and reserved

1¼ cups (300ml) Fish or Chicken Stock (see pages 30 and 28) or white wine

4 tbsp (50g) shallots, minced

2 garlic cloves, minced

a bouquet garni made with 4 sprigs of mint, 1 strip of lemon peel, and 1 sprig of lemon thyme (see page 30)

2–3 tbsp crème fraîche (optional)

lemon juice to taste

salt and freshly ground black pepper

1 Bring a pan of water to a boil and plunge in the watercress leaves. When the water reaches a boil again, remove the pan from the heat, drain the leaves, and refresh them immediately in ice water. Drain the leaves again and squeeze out the remaining water.

2 Pour the stock or wine into a small pan, add the shallots, garlic, watercress stems, and bouquet garni and bring to a boil. Reduce the heat and simmer gently until the liquid is reduced by half. Strain and reserve the liquid, discarding the vegetables.

3 Place the blanched watercress leaves and the strained reduction in a food processor or blender and process until smooth and creamy. For smoother results, strain the sauce after blending.

4 Return to a clean pan and heat very gently. Mix in the crème fraîche, if using, and heat for 1 minute, without letting the sauce boil. Season to taste and add the lemon juice just before serving.

CARROT COULIS

6 tbsp olive or peanut oil

1 tsp turmeric

1 tsp coriander seeds, freshly ground

1¾ cups (350g) carrots, chopped

1 tbsp honey

1¾ cups (400ml) Chicken or Vegetable Stock (see pages 28 and 31) or dry white wine

2 tbsp chopped cilantro

¼ tsp chili powder

2–3 tbsp lemon juice

finely grated lemon peel to taste (optional)

salt

A bright orange coulis with a spicy curry flavor that goes very well with cooked vegetables such as cauliflower and broccoli.

Advance preparation: the stock can be made in advance

Shelf life: 1 week in the refrigerator if made without the oil and lemon

1 Heat 4 tablespoons of the oil in a pan; add the turmeric and ground coriander and sauté for 1 minute. Add the carrots and honey; continue to cook until the carrots start to color, about 8 minutes.

2 Add the stock or wine, bring to a boil, and simmer for about 30 minutes, or until the carrots are very tender and the cooking liquid is reduced by about half.

3 Transfer the carrot mixture to a blender or food processor and purée to a smooth and creamy consistency.

4 Pour the mixture into a clean pan and bring to a boil. Remove from the heat; add the cilantro and chili powder and season with salt. Beat in the remaining 2 tablespoons of oil with the lemon juice and the optional grated peel. If a thinner consistency is preferred, stir in 1–2 tablespoons of stock or water.

AVOCADO COULIS

A creamy, smooth, piquant sauce that can be served either hot or cold. It is particularly good with fatty fish but also makes a surprisingly delicious pasta sauce.

Advance preparation: the stock can be made in advance

1¾ cups (400ml) Chicken Stock (see page 28)
⅓ cup (75g) shallots, finely chopped
1 small, ripe avocado, halved and flesh scooped out
2 tbsp lime juice
finely grated lime peel to taste
1 small red chili, seeded and finely chopped
3 tbsp heavy cream
salt

1 Put the stock and shallots in a small pan, bring to a boil; turn the heat to simmer and reduce the stock by half. Remove from the heat and set aside to cool.

2 Place the avocado flesh in a blender or food processor; add the cooled stock and the lime juice and process to a purée.

3 Transfer the mixture to a small pan and slowly heat to just below boiling point. Add the lime peel and chili and heat for a minute longer. Remove from the heat, add salt to taste, and beat in the cream.

FRESH TOMATO COULIS

Wonderfully versatile, this coulis can be served as a dip, used to add freshness to broiled fish or meat, or poured over pasta. It can also be flavored with thyme or lemon thyme.

Advance preparation: the tomato paste can be made in advance

Shelf life: 3 days in the refrigerator

See page 17 for illustration

1 recipe Tomato Paste (see page 43)
2 tbsp lemon juice
5–6 tbsp extra-virgin olive oil or hazelnut oil
2 tbsp chopped fresh basil, mint, flat-leaf parsley, or cilantro
salt and freshly ground black pepper

1 Place the tomato paste in a deep bowl and mix in the lemon juice. Beat in the oil a spoonful at a time.

2 Add the herbs, season to taste, and mix well. Chill before serving.

COOKED TOMATO COULIS

5 tbsp olive oil
⅓ cup (100g) shallots, finely chopped
3 garlic cloves, crushed
2lb (1kg) plum tomatoes, peeled, seeded, and chopped (see page 45)
a bouquet garni made with a few sprigs of thyme, 1 sprig of rosemary, a few celery leaves, 1 bay leaf, and 1 strip of lemon peel (see page 30)
1 tsp sugar or honey (optional)
2 tbsp chopped fresh basil, mint, oregano, or parsley (optional)
salt
freshly ground black pepper or 1 small red or green chili, chopped

1 Heat 3 tablespoons of the olive oil in a frying pan; add the shallots and garlic and sauté gently until the shallots are translucent, about 5 minutes.

2 Add the tomatoes and the bouquet garni and simmer over low heat for about 1 hour, stirring from time to time, until all the moisture has evaporated. Add the sugar or honey, if using.

3 Remove the bouquet garni; transfer the sauce to a blender or food processor and process until smooth.

4 Pour the sauce into a clean pan and bring to a boil, then remove from the heat and season to taste. Add the herbs, if using, and beat in the remaining 2 tablespoons of oil.

A simple and delicious tomato sauce that can be served as an accompaniment to vegetable dishes and broiled meat or fish, or tossed with pasta. Add a teaspoon of sugar or honey to enhance the tomatoes if they are a little bland. For extra flavor, beat in a little more olive oil just before serving. This sauce is so useful that it is worth making a large quantity and storing some for future use.

Shelf life: 1 week in the refrigerator; 3 months in the freezer

REDUCTION SAUCES

REDUCTION SAUCES are simply sauces based on stock that has been reduced by boiling to give an intense flavor. The classic reduction sauce is demi-glaze, which is worth mastering because it can form the base of many other wonderful sauces. One of the essential *haute-cuisine* sauces, it can take as long as two days to prepare because you need to make a rich stock first. Although the process can be time consuming, the results are always justifed, since a faithfully reduced sauce will be well-rounded, robust, and extremely flavorful.

DEMI-GLAZE

THIS LIGHTER AND HEALTHIER VERSION of the conventional demi-glaze uses no flour or Madeira, yet the finished sauce is clear, robust, and rich and can be served with red meat or used as a base for other sauces. Adding butter at the end gives the demi-glaze a wonderful rich gloss, but omit this and the seasoning if using the demi-glaze as a base for other sauces.

To save a little time, roughly chop the vegetables in a food processor rather than by hand. See opposite for richer, more conventional demi-glaze recipes.

Makes 1–1¼ cups (250–300ml)

2 tbsp olive oil

2 tbsp (30g) butter

¾ cup (150g) shallots, finely chopped

1 cup (200g) carrots, finely chopped

½ cup (100g) celery, finely chopped

1 cup (100g) leek, white part only, finely chopped

¾ cup (150g) very ripe tomatoes, peeled, seeded, and chopped (see page 43)

a bouquet garni made with 2 green leek leaves, 3 sprigs of thyme, 1 sprig of rosemary, a few sprigs of parsley, and 1 bay leaf (see page 30)

6 cups (1.5 liters) Brown Veal or Chicken Stock (see pages 29 and 28)

2 tbsp (30g) butter, chilled and cubed (optional)

salt, if necessary, and freshly ground black pepper (optional)

Shelf life: 1 week in the refrigerator

1 Heat the olive oil and butter in a large pan; add the shallots, carrots, celery, and leek and fry gently until lightly browned and caramelized.

2 Add the tomatoes, bouquet garni, and stock and bring to a boil. Reduce the heat and simmer, skimming off any residue from the surface, until the sauce is reduced by a third, about 45–50 minutes.

3 Strain the reduction through a sieve lined with cheesecloth. Transfer to a clean pan. Simmer the strained reduction for 45 minutes–1 hour, or until reduced by about three-quarters.

4 The finished demi-glaze should be thick and syrupy in consistency and evenly coat the back of a spoon. If the demi-glaze is to be served as a sauce, beat in the butter a little at a time, then season to taste.

MADEIRA DEMI-GLAZE

This is a richer version of the demi-glaze.

Advance preparation: the demi-glaze can be made in advance

Shelf life: 1 week in the refrigerator, although it is best served fresh

1 recipe Demi-glaze (see opposite)
⅓ cup + 2 tbsp (100ml) Madeira
2 tbsp (30g) butter, chilled and cubed
salt and freshly ground black pepper

1 Bring the demi-glaze and the Madeira slowly to a boil in a small pan. Reduce the heat to simmer and cook slowly, skimming any residue from the surface, until it has reduced by a third.

2 Remove from the heat, season to taste, and beat in the butter a little at a time.

VARIATION

RED DEMI-GLAZE

This is a decadent and wonderfully rich sauce that makes the perfect accompaniment to broiled steak.
• Bring 1 recipe Demi-glaze (see opposite) to a boil and add 1 cup (200ml) full-bodied red wine, such as Rioja, Shiraz, or Merlot. Reduce the heat to a simmer and add 3 sprigs of fresh thyme.
• Cook, skimming any residue from the surface, until it has reduced by half, about 30 minutes. Strain, season with salt and freshly ground pepper, and finish by beating in 2 tablespoons (30g) of chilled and cubed butter a little at a time as in the demi-glaze recipe.

JUNIPER DEMI-GLAZE

Robust and full of Mediterranean flavor, this sauce goes particularly well with pink roast lamb.

Advance preparation: the demi-glaze can be made in advance

Shelf life: 1 week in the refrigerator

See page 23 for illustration

1 recipe Demi-glaze (see opposite)
1 cup (200ml) full-bodied red wine such as Rioja, Shiraz, or Merlot
1 tbsp gin
2 small sprigs of rosemary
10 juniper berries, crushed
2 tbsp (30g) butter, chilled and cubed
salt and freshly ground black pepper

1 Bring the demi-glaze, wine, and gin to a boil in a pan. Reduce the heat and add the rosemary and juniper berries. Simmer, skimming any foam from the surface, until it has reduced by half.

2 Strain into a clean pan and return to a boil, then remove from the heat. Season and gradually beat in the butter.

THICKENED DEMI-GLAZE

4 tbsp (60g) clarified butter (see page 35)
¾ cup (150g) shallots, minced
1 cup (200g) carrots, finely chopped
½ cup (100g) celery, finely chopped
1 cup (100g) leeks, white part only, finely chopped
2–3 tbsp all-purpose flour, sifted
8 cups (2 liters) Brown Veal or Chicken Stock (see pages 29 and 28)
¾ cup (150g) very ripe tomatoes, peeled, seeded, and chopped (see page 43)
a bouquet garni made with 2 green leek leaves, 3 sprigs of thyme, 1 sprig of rosemary, a few sprigs of parsley, and 1 bay leaf (see page 30)
strained lemon juice to taste
salt and freshly ground black pepper

This is easier and relatively quicker to prepare than the modern Demi-glaze (see opposite). It is thickened with flour and therefore the reduction does not take as long. Although robust, this sauce does not have the intense flavor of the demi-glaze. Use instead of demi-glaze as a base for other sauces.

Advance preparation: the stock can be made in advance

1 Heat the butter in a large pan; add the shallots, carrots, celery, and leeks and fry gently until lightly browned, about 10–15 minutes. Sprinkle with the flour and cook, stirring continuously, until the flour starts to brown, about 5–8 minutes.

2 Add the stock and, stirring, bring to a boil, skimming any residue from the surface if necessary. Add the tomatoes and the bouquet garni and simmer until the stock has reduced by two-thirds.

3 Pour through a fine strainer or a strainer lined with cheesecloth. Season with salt and pepper and finish with a few drops of lemon juice.

WILD MUSHROOM DEMI-GLAZE

This is a wonderfully hearty and rich sauce that is perfect with steak.

Advance preparation: the demi-glaze can be made in advance

Shelf life: 1 week in the refrigerator if made without the butter

¼ cup (15g) dried porcini, soaked in ⅓ cup (75ml) hot water for 30 minutes
1 recipe Demi-glaze (see page 60)
¾ cup (200ml) red wine
2 sprigs of fresh thyme
1 garlic clove, finely chopped
2 tbsp (30g) butter, chilled and cubed
salt and freshly ground black pepper

1 Drain the porcini, reserving the soaking liquid, and chop finely. Put the demi-glaze, wine, and the strained porcini soaking liquid in a pan and slowly bring to a boil. Reduce the heat to minimum and add the porcini, thyme, and garlic. Simmer, skimming any foam from the surface, if necessary, until reduced by half.

2 Strain into a clean pan and bring back to a boil. Turn off the heat, season, and stir in the butter a little at a time.

RED WINE SAUCE

This sauce of Eastern European origin is especially good with poached or fried carp. It also goes well with salmon and bass and with freshwater fish such as trout.

Advance preparation: the stock can be made in advance

Shelf life: 1 week in the refrigerator if made without the butter

1 tbsp virgin olive oil or peanut oil
⅓ cup (75g) shallots, finely chopped
⅓ cup (75g) carrots, finely chopped
1 inch (2.5cm) piece ginger, shredded
1 tbsp honey
2½ cups (500ml) Fish Stock, made with red wine (see page 30)
⅔ cup (300ml) fruity red wine
2 tsp sweet Hungarian paprika
¼ tsp hot Hungarian paprika or cayenne pepper
lemon juice to taste
¼ tsp grated lemon peel
2 tbsp (75g) butter, chilled and cubed
salt and freshly ground black pepper

1 Heat the oil in a small pan; add the shallots, carrots, ginger, and honey and fry, stirring frequently, until the shallots turn golden and begins to caramelize. Add the stock and wine and bring to a boil, then reduce the heat and bubble gently, skimming any foam from the surface if necessary, until the sauce is reduced by two-thirds, about 25 minutes.

2 Pour the sauce through a strainer into a clean pan; add the sweet paprika and the hot paprika or cayenne pepper, and bring to a boil. Reduce the heat and allow to simmer for 10 minutes.

3 Season to taste and add the lemon juice and peel. Remove from the heat and stir in the butter a little at a time just before serving.

ORANGE & SAFFRON SAUCE ▷

strained juice of 3 oranges
1¾ cups (400ml) Fish Stock (see page 30)
¼ tsp saffron strands, soaked in a little warm fish stock or water
½ tsp cornstarch, dissolved in 1 tbsp orange juice or water
thinly pared peel of 1 orange, cut into fine julienne
a few drops of lemon juice
½ tsp finely chopped red chili or ½ tsp cayenne pepper
2 tbsp (75g) butter, chilled and cubed
salt

A superbly fragrant sauce that is especially good with strong-flavored fish, such as red or gray mullet or tuna.

Advance preparation: the stock can be made in advance

Shelf life: 3–4 days in the refrigerator if made without the butter

1 Place the orange juice and stock in a pan and bring to a boil. Reduce the heat and simmer gently, skimming any residue from the surface, if necessary, until it is reduced by two thirds, about 25 minutes.

2 Add the saffron, cornstarch, and orange peel and beat for about a minute until the sauce has thickened slightly. Add the lemon juice and chili or cayenne. Simmer for 2 minutes, then remove from the heat, beat in the butter a little at a time, season with salt, and serve immediately.

OPPOSITE: RED MULLET IN A TANGY ORANGE AND SAFFRON SAUCE

GINGER & SCALLION SAUCE

An interesting marriage of East and West, this piquant sauce is especially good with salmon.

Advance preparation: the stock can be made in advance

Shelf life: 3 days in the refrigerator if made without the butter

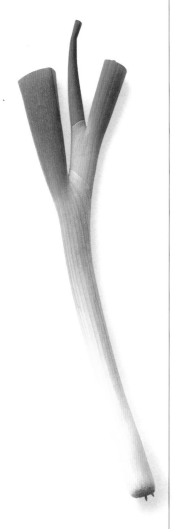

4 large (125g) scallions
2 tbsp (30g) butter
1 tbsp all-purpose flour
1 tbsp Cooked Tomato Coulis (see page 59) or 1 tsp Tomato Paste (see page 43) or 1 tsp canned tomato paste
1¾ cups (400ml) Fish Stock (see page 30)
½ inch (1cm) ginger, minced
2 tbsp lemon juice
cayenne pepper to taste
5 tbsp (75g) butter, chilled and cubed
salt

1 Finely chop the white part of the scallions. Chop 4 or 5 of the tender green tops into pieces and set aside.

2 Heat the butter in a small pan; add the scallions and sauté gently until they begin to color. Sprinkle in the flour and sauté for 2 minutes, then add the tomato coulis or paste and cook for about 1 minute or so, stirring frequently.

3 Add the stock, beating to incorporate any bits from the bottom of the pan, and bring to a boil. Reduce the heat and simmer gently, skimming any foam from the surface, if necessary, until the sauce is reduced by half, about 25 minutes. Stir often to prevent sticking.

4 Strain the sauce through a sieve into a clean pan, using the back of a spoon to press through as much of the onion as possible. Add the ginger and simmer for 1–2 minutes, then remove from the heat and add the lemon juice. Season with cayenne pepper and salt to taste. Beat in the butter a few pieces at a time; add the chopped scallion tops and serve immediately.

LEMON SAUCE

1¾ cups (400ml) Fish Stock (see page 30)
strained juice and finely grated peel of 1 small lemon
½ tsp sugar or honey
1 tsp cornstarch, dissolved in 1 tbsp white wine or water
½ or 1 small preserved lemon, rinsed, pulp removed and skin finely chopped
1 small red chili, chopped (optional)
7 tbsp (100g) butter, chilled and cubed
salt and freshly ground black pepper

1 Put the stock, lemon juice, and sugar or honey in a pan and bring to a boil. Reduce the heat and bubble very gently, skimming any foam from the surface, if necessary, until reduced by two-thirds.

2 Add the cornstarch and stir until the mixture has thickened slightly. Add the lemon peel, the preserved lemon, and the chili, if using, and simmer for 2–3 minutes. Remove from the heat; beat in the butter a little at a time, then season to taste.

Moroccan preserved lemon lends this refreshing sauce a delightfully tart, piquant flavor. It is especially good with broiled red mullet or broiled fatty fish such as mackerel, but if you substitute chicken stock for the fish stock it also makes a good sauce for chicken. Preserved lemons are available in Middle Eastern and Mediterranean shops.

Advance preparation: the stock can be made in advance

Shelf life: 1 week in the refrigerator if made without the butter

BALSAMIC VINEGAR SAUCE

1¾ cups (400ml) Fish Stock, made with red wine (see page 30)
⅓ cup (100ml) aged balsamic vinegar
1 tsp cornstarch, dissolved in 1 tbsp balsamic vinegar
7 tbsp (100g) butter, chilled and cubed
salt and freshly ground black pepper

1 Bring the stock and balsamic vinegar to a boil in a small pan. Reduce the heat and simmer gently for 15–20 minutes, skimming any foam from the surface when necessary, until reduced by two-thirds.

2 Increase the heat, add the cornstarch and boil for 1 minute until thickened. Beat in the butter a little at a time, then season to taste with salt and freshly ground black pepper. Serve immediately.

Simple and quick, this sauce makes a memorable dish when served with salmon, trout, or sea bass.

Advance preparation: the stock can be made in advance

Shelf life: 1 week in the refrigerator if made without the butter

GRAVIES

THE WORD "GRAVY" comes via France from a Latin word meaning made with grain. It describes a sauce formed by thickening and deglazing pan juices after roasting meat. A lighter, more contemporary sauce can be made by omitting the flour and simmering the gravy for a few minutes longer. It is important to make the sauce in a roasting pan, since its large surface area helps the process of evaporation and thickening.

TRADITIONAL PAN GRAVY

This is made from the pan juices left behind after cooking a roast.

Advance preparation: the stock can be made in advance

Shelf life: 1 week in the refrigerator

1–2 tbsp all-purpose flour or ½–1 tbsp cornstarch
2 cups (500ml) Brown or Chicken Stock (see pages 29 and 28) or ½ red or white wine and ½ stock
2–3 tbsp chopped fresh parsley (optional)
salt and freshly ground black pepper

1 Remove the roast meat or poultry from the roasting pan and let it rest in a warm place. Drain off all but 2 tablespoons of the fat that has collected in the bottom of the pan.

2 Place the roasting pan on top of the stove over low heat and sprinkle in the flour or cornstarch. Cook for 3–4 minutes, stirring continuously and scraping any residue from the bottom of the pan.

3 Add the stock and bring to a boil, stirring, then simmer for about 5–8 minutes, until the gravy has thickened slightly. Season, add the parsley, if using, and serve in a gravy boat with the meat.

VARIATIONS

GRAVY FOR LAMB OR GAME
Follow the recipe above, but use 1½ cups (350ml) stock and ⅔ cup (150ml) port.

TOMATO GRAVY *See page 17 for illustration*
Follow the recipe above, but add 1¼ cups (75g) chopped sun-dried tomatoes and 1 tablespoon of Tomato Paste (see page 43) or canned tomato paste just before adding the flour. This is delicious with roast lamb or chicken.

MUSTARD GRAVY
Follow the recipe above, but, before serving, stir in 1 heaped tablespoon of grainy mustard. Serve with chicken.

ONION GRAVY

4 tbsp (60g) butter
1lb (500g) onions, halved and thinly sliced
1 tbsp all-purpose flour
3¼ cups (750ml) Brown Stock (see page 29)
1 tbsp lemon juice
¼ tsp cayenne pepper or a few drops of Tabasco sauce
salt and freshly ground black pepper

This sweet and comforting gravy is especially good with sausages, or simply poured over mashed potatoes, roasted meat, or poultry.

Advance preparation: the stock can be made in advance

Shelf life: 1 week in the refrigerator

1 Heat the butter in a pan; add the onions and sauté over medium heat until they are soft and translucent, about 10–15 minutes.

2 Sprinkle with the flour and cook for about 3 minutes, scraping the bottom of the pan and stirring continuously.

3 Add the stock and bring to a boil, then reduce the heat and simmer until reduced by half. Add the lemon juice and the cayenne pepper or Tabasco, season to taste, and serve.

VARIATION

CARAMELIZED ONION GRAVY
For a sweeter, richer, more intensely flavored onion gravy, follow the recipe above, but cook the onions for 40–50 minutes, or until evenly browned and thickened. Finish as from step 2.

DRESSINGS

HERE IS AN INSPIRATIONAL COLLECTION OF RECIPES THAT ARE BOTH EASY AND FUN TO PREPARE. GATHERED

FROM ALL CORNERS OF THE WORLD, THESE DRESSINGS CAN BE DRIZZLED OVER SALADS, BUT THEIR FLAVORS

AND SIMPLICITY MAKE THEM VERSATILE. TRY USING THEM AS SANDWICH SPREADS, SPOONING THEM

OVER STEAMED OR BOILED VEGETABLES, OR POURING THEM OVER BROILED MEAT OR FISH.

BLUE CHEESE DRESSING

For a version with fewer calories, use ⅔ cup (150ml) low-fat or fat-free yogurt instead of mayonnaise.

Advance preparation: *the mayonnaise can be made in advance*

Shelf life: *1 week in the refrigerator*

1 recipe Mayonnaise
(see pages 38–39)

1¼ cups (150g) blue cheese, such as Danish blue, gorgonzola, or dolcelatte, crumbled

2 tbsp white wine vinegar

salt, if necessary, and freshly ground black pepper

Place all the ingredients in a food processor and process until smooth.

THOUSAND ISLAND DRESSING

One of the more famous salad dressings, this can also be served over hard-boiled eggs or as a dip for crudités. If using tomato ketchup, remember to enliven the sauce with a pinch of cayenne, chili powder, or a few drops of Tabasco.

Advance preparation: *the mayonnaise can be made in advance*

Shelf life: *1 week in the refrigerator*

1 recipe Mayonnaise
(see pages 38–39)

4 tbsp mild chili sauce or tomato ketchup

1 hard-boiled egg, finely chopped

2 tbsp finely chopped stuffed green olives

1 tbsp finely chopped onion

1 tbsp finely chopped green pepper

1 tbsp finely chopped sour pickle

1 tbsp snipped fresh chives

1 tbsp lemon or lime juice

salt and freshly ground black pepper

Mix all the ingredients together in a bowl.

FETA CHEESE DRESSING

¾ cup (100g) crumbled feta cheese

2 tbsp lemon juice

1 garlic clove, crushed

1 tsp grated lemon peel

4 tbsp extra-virgin olive oil

3 tbsp chopped fresh mint or flat-leaf parsley

freshly ground black pepper

Creamy, sharp, and delicious, this dressing goes particularly well with tomato and onion salad, but can also be served as a dip or poured over rice or pasta.

Shelf life: *1 week in the refrigerator*

Place all the ingredients except the mint or parsley in a food processor and process until smooth. Add the mint or parsley and process briefly to mix.

MANGO DRESSING ▷

1 ripe mango, peeled and pitted

juice of 2 limes or 1 lemon

1 tbsp Dijon or English mustard

1 tsp grated lemon or lime peel

1 small chili, seeded and finely chopped

2 tbsp snipped fresh chives

salt and freshly ground black pepper

A delicious fat-free dressing to serve over green salad or as a sauce for broiled fish or meat. Add a little sugar if necessary to balance the flavors. Stirring in the peel, chili, and chives at the end keeps the texture consistent.

Shelf life: *1 week in the refrigerator*

Process the mango flesh and lime or lemon juice in a food processor until smooth. If the mango is stringy, press the purée through a strainer. Transfer to a bowl and stir in the remaining ingredients.

OPPOSITE: SNIPPED FRESH CHIVES BEING STIRRED INTO MANGO DRESSING

SOUR CREAM DRESSING

This is a popular topping for baked potatoes and green salads. For a low-calorie version, substitute low-fat or fat-free yogurt for the sour cream.

Shelf life: 1 week in the refrigerator

⅔ cup (150ml) thick sour cream or fromage frais
1–2 tbsp lemon juice, white wine vinegar, or cider vinegar
1 tsp Dijon mustard (optional)
2 tbsp snipped fresh chives, dill, or flat-leaf parsley
salt and freshly ground white or black pepper

Mix all the ingredients together in a bowl.

TAHINI SAUCE

A versatile Middle Eastern sauce that is served as a dip with pita bread or as a salad dressing. For a richer flavor, mix in 2–3 tablespoons of extra-virgin olive oil just before serving. To use this as a cooking sauce, add 1 cup (250ml) milk or water; then pour over cooked vegetables or broiled fish and bake or broil until golden.

Shelf life: 1 week in the refrigerator (omit the garlic and add just before serving)

1 cup (250g) tahini
strained juice of 2 lemons, or to taste
¾ cup (175ml) water
1 garlic clove, crushed (optional)
2–3 tbsp chopped fresh flat-leaf parsley or mint (optional)
salt

1 Mix the tahini and lemon juice together in a small bowl. The mixture will separate and may appear lumpy at first, but continue to mix, adding small quantities of the water, and it will soon reach the consistency of heavy cream.

2 Add the rest of the ingredients and mix well. Alternatively, put all the ingredients except the herbs, if using, in a food processor and process to a smooth cream. Add the herbs.

VARIATIONS

HAZELNUT OR PEANUT TAHINI
Follow the recipe above, but substitute 1 cup (200g) hazelnut butter (available from natural food stores) or peanut butter for the tahini.

GREEN TAHINI
This is a bright green, fresh-tasting version of tahini that can be made in a food processor or blender. Follow the recipe above but omit the parsley or mint. Process 7 cups (100g) fresh flat-leaf parsley, mint, or dill, or a mixture of all three, with 3 tablespoons tahini sauce until smooth, 1–2 minutes. With the machine running, add the remaining tahini sauce and process to blend.

SALAD DRESSING

1 tbsp dry mustard
2 tbsp all-purpose flour or cornstarch
1–2 tbsp sugar, or to taste
3 egg yolks
1 cup (250ml) light cream, heavy cream, or milk
⅖ cup (100ml) cider vinegar or white wine vinegar
salt

This sauce is easy to make, has less fat than mayonnaise, and keeps very well. Similar to making custard, salad dressing should be stirred continuously and never allowed to boil.

Shelf life: 1 week in the refrigerator

1 Mix the mustard, flour, sugar, and egg yolks together in a bowl. Gradually add the cream or milk, beating well.

2 Place the bowl over a pan of barely simmering water, not letting the bottom of the bowl touch the water, and stir until it starts to thicken. Add the vinegar and salt and cook until thick and smooth.

VINAIGRETTE

2 tsp Dijon mustard
1 tbsp honey (optional)
2 tbsp wine vinegar, cider vinegar, or other flavored vinegar, or lemon or lime juice
6–8 tbsp virgin olive oil
salt and freshly ground black pepper

Vinaigrette is one of the simplest and most versatile sauces. Use it to dress salads or to complement dry, cured meats, or pour it over broiled fish as a sauce. I like to drizzle it over pasta, bulgur, couscous, or rice for a fast and satisfying meal.

Shelf life: 3 weeks refrigerated in a screw-top jar

In a bowl, beat together the mustard, honey, vinegar, or lemon or lime juice and seasoning. Gradually add the oil, beating constantly, until the sauce is smooth and thick. Alternatively, put all the ingredients in a screw-top jar and shake well to mix.

VARIATIONS

ROQUEFORT DRESSING
I drizzle this over salads as well as broiled steak and lamb chops. Follow the recipe above, but mix the vinaigrette in a blender or food processor and add ½ cup (60g) crumbled Roquefort cheese.

GARLIC & HERB VINAIGRETTE
Follow the recipe above, but add 1 crushed garlic clove and 1–2 tablespoons chopped fresh parsley, coriander, chives, or tarragon.

PEPPER & CHILI VINAIGRETTE

A vinaigrette for chili lovers. You can also use canned roasted peppers.

Shelf life: *1 week in the refrigerator*

1 recipe Vinaigrette made with lemon or lime juice (see opposite)
2 tbsp finely chopped roasted and peeled red pepper (see page 96)
½ tsp grated lemon or lime peel
1–2 green or red chilies, seeded and finely chopped
1–2 tbsp chopped cilantro

Mix all the ingredients together in a bowl.

COOKED VINAIGRETTE

This sauce is based on a recipe by Nico Ladenis, one of London's most innovative chefs. In the original recipe, the vinaigrette is strained and the vegetables are discarded. I like to leave the vegetables in the vinaigrette and serve it as a textured sauce with vegetables, fish, or meat. It's not really worth making this in small quantities, especially since it keeps so well.

Makes 6¼ cups (1.5 liters)

Shelf life: *1 month in the refrigerator; 6 months in a sealed jar (see pages 134–35)*

See page 23 for illustration

4 cups (1 liter) olive oil
⅓ cup (100ml) white wine vinegar
1 tbsp honey (optional)
1½ cups (350ml) dry white wine
⅔ cup (100g) carrots, finely chopped
½ cup (100g) celery, finely chopped
½ cup (100g) red bell pepper, finely chopped
½ cup (100g) shallots, finely chopped
5 garlic cloves, finely chopped
a bouquet garni made with 4 sprigs of thyme, 2 sprigs of rosemary, 2 strips of lemon peel, and 2 bay leaves (see page 30)
1 tsp black peppercorns and ½ tsp cloves, tied in a cheesecloth square
¾ cup (150g) plum tomatoes, skinned, seeded (see page 43), and finely chopped
1 tsp salt

1 Heat the oil, vinegar, and honey, if using, in a pan. Add the rest of the ingredients and bring to a boil. Reduce the heat to minimum and simmer for about 30 minutes, skimming any foam from the surface if necessary.

2 Remove the bouquet garni and, if desired, strain through a cheesecloth-lined strainer to remove the vegetables.

STEVE'S SPICY VINAIGRETTE

⅓ cup (100ml) fresh orange juice
strained juice of ½ lemon
6 tbsp olive oil
1 tbsp honey
1 tbsp Dijon mustard
1 tsp grated ginger
½ tsp grated orange peel
salt and freshly ground black pepper

This recipe was given to me by my good friend Steve. Spicy and intense in flavor, this recipe makes a superb dressing for cooked or raw celery root. It is also delicious with fish or as a simple sauce for broiled duck or game birds.

Shelf life: *1 week in the refrigerator*

1 Simmer the orange and lemon juice in a small pan until reduced to about 3 tablespoons; then set aside to cool.

2 Transfer the cooled mixture to a bowl and stir in the oil, honey, and mustard. Mix in the ginger, orange peel, and seasoning.

RASPBERRY VINAIGRETTE

2 tbsp raspberry vinegar or red wine vinegar
1 tsp honey
⅓ cup (2oz) fresh raspberries
6 tbsp olive or hazelnut oil
1 tbsp snipped fresh chervil or flat-leaf parsley
salt and freshly ground black pepper

Bright red, refreshing, and tart, this is especially good served cold or warmed slightly, drizzled over duck or chicken salad, broiled goat's cheese, plain broiled poultry, or fish.

Shelf life: *1 week in the refrigerator*

See page 21 for illustration

Mix the vinegar and honey together in a bowl. Crush the raspberries to a pulp with a fork, then whisk them into the vinegar mixture along with the oil, chervil or parsley, and seasoning.

WARM MAPLE VINAIGRETTE

3 tbsp cider vinegar
3 tbsp maple syrup
1 tsp English mustard
8 tbsp olive or walnut oil
salt and freshly ground black pepper

A sweet and sour dressing that is excellent with broiled chicken or chicken salad, or simply spooned over steamed vegetables.

Shelf life: *1 week in the refrigerator*

Warm the vinegar and maple syrup in a small pan. Stir in the mustard and the oil, season to taste, and serve warm.

FLAVORED OILS

A FEW DROPS OF FLAVORED OIL in a stew or sauce can add instant color, fragrance, and interest. Drizzle a couple of tablespoons over pasta and sprinkle with fresh herbs for a fast, convenient, and delicious meal. Unless specified otherwise in the recipe, use light, well-filtered, and refined oil, such as peanut, sesame, vegetable, or soy; cold-pressed virgin oils have a strong taste that might overpower more subtle flavorings. Oils that contain raw ingredients should be stored in sterilized jars (see pages 134–35).

HERB OIL

I use herb-flavored oils in salad dressings or, added at the last minute, to flavor soups and stews. Try herbs such as basil, thyme, and rosemary, and experiment with different combinations.

Shelf life: *3 weeks unfiltered; 6 months filtered*

See page 11 for illustration

| 4 cups (1 liter) light olive oil |
| 7 cups (200g) fresh herb leaves |

Heat the oil to 104°F/40°C in a pan. Lightly bruise the herbs; then put them in a sterilized bottle or jar (see pages 134–35). Pour the warm oil over the herbs and seal. Store in a cool, dark place for 2–3 weeks, shaking the container occasionally. The oil can now be used but lasts longer if it is filtered and the herbs discarded (see pages 134–35).

VARIATION

LAVENDER OIL
Lavender is a wonderful, aromatic flavoring for oil and is also very easy to grow. Add this oil to salad dressings or sauces, or drizzle it over steamed vegetables. Follow the recipe above, but use 4 cups (1 liter) almond or peanut oil instead of olive oil. Substitute 4 cups (200–300g) lavender flowerheads for the herbs.

THAI CARAMELIZED OIL

A wonderfully piquant and fragrant oil with a pronounced flavor of shallots and garlic. Add to salad dressings, or use to give a caramelized onion flavor to mashed potatoes.

Shelf life: *6 months (sealed and refrigerated, the fried shallot mix can be stored for up to 1 month and used to dress salads or to add texture to soups and stews)*

| ¾ cup (150g) shallots, chopped |
| 10 garlic cloves, chopped |
| 2 inch piece (5cm) ginger, grated |
| 1–2 Thai chilies or fresh or dried bird's eye chilies, crushed |
| 4 cups (1 liter) oil |

Gently sauté all the ingredients in the oil until the shallots are golden and just beginning to brown, about 15–20 minutes. Remove from the heat and allow to cool. The oil is ready for use or can be filtered into a sterilized bottle (see pages 134–35).

LEMON OIL

| 4 cups (1 liter) oil |
| thinly grated peel of 5 lemons, all white pith removed |

Be sure to use unwaxed lemons for this oil.

Shelf life: *6 months*

Put the oil in a pan and warm to 140°F/60°C. Place the lemon peel in a sterilized jar or bottle (see pages 134–35), pour in the oil, and seal. Keep the container in a warm place for about a week, shaking the bottle occasionally. Filter the oil into a sterilized bottle (see pages 134–35).

GARLIC OIL

| 4 heads of fresh garlic, cut across into halves |
| 4–5 sprigs of fresh thyme |
| 4 cups (1 liter) light olive oil |

The garlic may be roasted before being immersed in oil to give a nuttier, milder flavor. Simply place it in a roasting tin, sprinkle with a little oil, and roast for 25–30 minutes, or until soft. The marinated garlic is wonderful in salsas and salads.

Shelf life: *6 months*

Place the garlic and thyme in a sterilized bottle or jar (see pages 134–35), cover with the oil, and seal tightly. Sterilize the sealed bottle and store in a warm place for 2–3 weeks. The oil is then ready to use, or it can be filtered and saved for future use (see pages 134–35).

FRESH CHILI OIL ▷

Hot, fragrant, and wonderfully mellow, chili oil can be used to dress pasta, salads, or broiled fish or meat; I even use it as a barbecue sauce. For decorative effect, add whole chilies to the oil after filtering – especially if giving a bottle of this as a gift.

Shelf life: 6 months

2 (300g) red or green chilies, stems removed, sliced in half
4–5 sprigs of fresh thyme
4 cups (1 liter) oil

1 Place the chilies, thyme, and oil in a saucepan and bring to a simmer. Reduce the heat and allow to cook gently for about 15 minutes.

2 Pour into a sterilized bottle (see pages 134–35), seal, and allow to stand for 2 weeks to develop flavor. Filter the oil and re-sterilize the bottle (see pages 134–35).

SMOKY CHILI OIL

If you include bird's eye chilies this mild oil becomes a hot favorite for the chili lover.

Shelf life: 6 months

1 cup (50g) chipotle chilies, stems removed, coarsely crushed
1 cup (50g) guindila chilies, stalks removed, coarsely crushed
1 tbsp bird's eye chilies (optional), stalks removed, coarsely crushed
4 cups (1 liter) oil

Gently heat all the ingredients in a pan, but do not allow the oil to get hotter than 212°F/100°C. Simmer for 20 minutes; then remove from the heat and allow to cool. The oil is ready for use immediately or it can be filtered, bottled, and sterilized (see pages 134–35).

KAFFIR LIME OIL

A superbly fragrant and versatile oil. Use it to flavor vinaigrettes and mayonnaises and to drizzle over either raw vegetables or thinly sliced smoked meats and fish.

Shelf life: 6 months

4 cups (1 liter) oil
thinly pared peel of 4 limes, all white pith removed
20 kaffir lime leaves

Warm the oil to 140°F/60°C, making sure that it does not get any hotter. Lightly bruise the peel and the leaves and put into a sterilized bottle or jar. Pour in the warm oil and seal. Store in a cool, dark place for 2–3 weeks; then filter and re-sterilize the bottle (see pages 134–35).

RIGHT: FRESH CHILI OIL BEING POURED INTO A JAR

MAYONNAISE

The master recipe for making mayonnaise, including instructions for making it in a food processor, is on pages 38–39.

Shelf life: *1 week in the refrigerator*

2 egg yolks, at cool room temperature
2 tsp lemon juice or white wine vinegar, plus a little extra to taste
1 tsp Dijon mustard or dry mustard
a small pinch of salt
1¼ cups (300ml) peanut, light olive, or light, flavorless oil such as sesame
salt and freshly ground black pepper

In a bowl, mix together the egg yolks, lemon juice or vinegar, mustard and salt. Beating continuously, start adding the oil a drop at a time until about one-third has been amalgamated. Continuing to beat, pour in the rest of the oil in a thin, steady stream until the mayonnaise is thick and glossy. Stir in lemon juice or vinegar and salt and freshly ground black pepper to taste.

VARIATIONS

GARLIC MAYONNAISE
This is delicious as a dip or served with fish, cold chicken, or steamed vegetables. Follow the recipe above, using lemon juice rather than vinegar. Mash 4–6 garlic cloves to a paste with a little salt and mix this into the finished mayonnaise, along with 2 tablespoons chopped fresh herbs, such as thyme, oregano, mint, parsley, dill, or marjoram. Season with salt and freshly ground pepper.

HERB MAYONNAISE
Serve this with fish or as a salad dressing. Stir 3 tablespoons Herb Purée (see page 42) and 1 tablespoon lemon juice into the finished mayonnaise. Season to taste.

SMOKY RED PEPPER MAYONNAISE
Roast, peel, and purée 2 red peppers (see page 96); place them in a cheesecloth-lined strainer and drain for 2 hours. Stir the drained purée and 2 tablespoons lemon juice into the finished mayonnaise. Season with salt and black pepper.

ORANGE MUSTARD MAYONNAISE
This is delicious with poached fish, especially salmon. Bring the juice of 3 oranges to a boil in a small pan and simmer for 15–20 minutes until reduced to about ⅓ cup (75ml). Remove from the heat and allow to cool; then mix into the finished mayonnaise along with the grated peel of 1 orange, 1 tablespoon lemon juice, and 3–4 tablespoons grainy mustard such as *moutarde de meaux*. Season to taste with salt and freshly ground black pepper.

BEET MAYONNAISE
Purée ½ cup (100g) chopped, cooked beets and 2 tablespoons red or white wine vinegar in a food processor. Press the purée through a strainer; then stir it into the finished mayonnaise and season with salt and freshly ground black pepper.

HARISSA MAYONNAISE
For a chili-spiked mayonnaise, stir 3–4 tablespoons Harissa (see page 103) into the finished mayonnaise.

SHRIMP COCKTAIL SAUCE
Make this classic sauce by stirring 4 tablespoons tomato ketchup, 1 tablespoon Worcestershire sauce, 1 tablespoon lemon juice, and Tabasco or cayenne pepper to taste into the finished mayonnaise. Season with salt and freshly ground pepper.

GREEN GODDESS DRESSING *See page 11 for illustration*
This classic American sauce, created in the 1920s by the chef at San Francisco's Palace Hotel, is wonderful served with steak or broiled fish. Stir ⅓ cup (100ml) sour cream, 4 finely chopped scallions, 4 finely chopped anchovy fillets, 3 tablespoons finely chopped fresh parsley, and 2 tablespoons tarragon vinegar into the finished mayonnaise. Season to taste with salt and freshly ground black pepper.

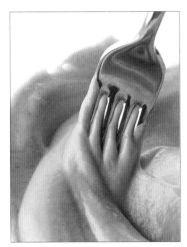

HERB MAYONNAISE   SMOKY RED PEPPER MAYONNAISE   ORANGE MUSTARD MAYONNAISE   BEET MAYONNAISE

GRIBICHE

A delicious version of mayonnaise that goes well with fish or hard-boiled eggs; it also makes a very good dip for raw or steamed vegetables.

Shelf life: 1 week in the refrigerator

3 hard-boiled egg yolks
1 raw egg yolk
1 tbsp Dijon mustard
1 cup (250ml) olive oil
1 tbsp white wine vinegar
3 hard-boiled egg whites, chopped or coarsely grated
2 tbsp capers, chopped
2 tbsp cornichons or sour pickles, chopped
2 tbsp chopped fresh *fines herbes* (chervil, chives, parsley, tarragon)
salt and freshly ground black pepper

Either press the hard-boiled egg yolks through a sieve into a bowl or mash with a fork. Add the raw egg yolk and mustard and mix to make a smooth paste. Start adding the oil in a trickle, whisking continuously, until half the oil has been added. Mix in the vinegar and, still whisking, slowly add the rest of the oil. The sauce should be thick and shiny. Add the rest of the ingredients and mix well.

VARIATION

TARTARE SAUCE

Follow the recipe above, but omit the egg whites and the cornichons or pickles. Increase the quantity of capers to 3 tablespoons, add ¼ cup (60g) finely chopped onion or shallots and use finely chopped parsley instead of the *fines herbes*.

AÏOLI

4–6 garlic cloves
¼ tsp salt
2 hard-boiled egg yolks, pressed through a fine strainer
1 raw egg yolk
1¼ cups (300ml) olive oil
lemon juice

Put the garlic and salt in a food processor and purée to a smooth paste. Add the boiled and the raw egg yolks and process to mix. With the machine running, start adding the oil a drop at a time, then in a thin, steady stream. Finish by adding lemon juice to taste, pulsing briefly to mix.

A classic French sauce so called because of the large quantity of garlic (ail) that is used to make it. Some recipes recommend using up to 2 garlic cloves per person, which produces a highly flavored, pungent sauce.

Shelf life: 1 week in the refrigerator

RÉMOULADE

1 recipe Mayonnaise (see opposite)
1 tbsp finely chopped pickle
1 tbsp finely chopped capers
1 tbsp each chopped fresh parsley, chervil, and tarragon
1 tbsp Dijon mustard
3–4 anchovy fillets, finely chopped

Mix all the ingredients together in a bowl.

Serve this with fish or cold meats or as a dip for steamed vegetables.

Advance preparation: the mayonnaise can be made in advance

Shelf life: 1 week in the refrigerator

YOGURTTAISE

A lighter version of traditional mayonnaise with many fewer calories. For extra body and a creamier texture, drain the yogurt and fromage frais beforehand: pour each one into a separate cheesecloth-lined strainer over a bowl and let them drain in the refrigerator for 5–6 hours.

¾ cup (200ml) yogurt, well chilled
¾ cup (200ml) fromage frais, well chilled
1 tbsp Dijon or English mustard
strained juice of 1 lemon
grated peel of ½ lemon (optional)
⅓ cup (75ml) olive, peanut, or hazelnut oil
salt and freshly ground black pepper

BY HAND: combine the yogurt, fromage frais, mustard, lemon juice, and peel, if using, in a bowl. Whisk in a few drops of the oil. Pour in a little more oil and, continuing to whisk, gradually add the rest of it until the mixture is glossy and thickly coats the back of a spoon. Season to taste with salt and black pepper.

MACHINE METHOD: put all the ingredients except the oil in a food processor. With the machine on high speed, slowly add the oil in a thin, steady stream.

Shelf life: 1 week in the refrigerator

FLAVORED BUTTERS

THESE BUTTERS OFFER A FAST AND INNOVATIVE way of adding instant flavor to a whole host of dishes. Spread over bread, they transform canapés and sandwiches. Stirred into sauces and stews in the final cooking stages, they enhance the texture and flavor. The butters can be served with roasted meats, chicken, or fish. Melted, they make wonderful dipping sauces for shrimp or steamed vegetables, for example.

Traditionally, the ingredients are pounded in a mortar and pestle, but using a food processor or blender makes the process very quick and easy. I like a textured butter, but for smoother results, rub the butter through a drum sieve with the help of a plastic scraper. Flavored butters are best eaten fresh, but tightly wrapped they do keep well, and, for convenience, I always have one or two varieties in my refrigerator or freezer.

CHILI BUTTER

This is especially good with barbecued or broiled fish and chicken.

Shelf life: 1 week in the refrigerator; 1 month in the freezer

1 red pepper, roasted, peeled, and seeded (see page 96)
1 cup (200g) unsalted butter, softened
1 tbsp lemon juice
1–2 red or green chilies or a mixture, seeded and very finely chopped
1 tbsp finely chopped cilantro (optional)
salt

1 Purée the pepper in a blender or food processor. Pour the purée into a cheesecloth-lined strainer over a bowl and set aside to drain for 1 hour.

2 Place the butter in a bowl; add the drained pepper purée and the lemon juice and beat until light and fluffy. Mix in the chili and the cilantro, if using, and add salt to taste. Roll (see below) and chill until firm.

ROLLING BUTTER

1 Divide the butter into halves and place on a piece of waxed paper, foil, or plastic wrap.

2 Roll each one into an even sausage shape and secure by twisting the ends.

LEMONGRASS & LIME BUTTER

1 cup (200g) unsalted butter, softened
4 lemongrass stalks, hard outer layers removed, finely chopped or pounded
2 tbsp lime juice
salt
1 small chili, seeded and finely chopped (optional)
5 kaffir lime leaves, finely shredded

An exceptionally fresh and fragrant butter that will add a wonderful aromatic tanginess to seafood or fish; it can also be spread on bread or used in canapés.

Shelf life: 1 week in the refrigerator; 1 month in the freezer

1 Heat ½ cup (100g) of the butter in a small pan, add the lemongrass and sauté gently until it begins to color. Remove from the heat and set aside to cool, then strain through a cheesecloth-lined strainer.

2 In a bowl, beat the remaining butter until light and fluffy. Add the strained butter and the rest of the ingredients and mix well. Roll (see left) and chill until firm.

TOMATO BUTTER

¾ cup (100g) sun-dried tomatoes in oil, well drained
1 cup (200g) unsalted butter, softened
2 tbsp shredded fresh basil
salt and freshly ground black pepper

This is delicious on canapés or on bread. For a more textured butter, purée half the tomatoes and coarsely chop the rest by hand before adding to the butter.

Shelf life: 1 week in the refrigerator; 1 month in the freezer

Purée the tomatoes in a food processor or blender, then add the butter and blend well. Add the basil and season with salt, if necessary, and pepper. Roll (see left) and chill until firm.

ANCHOVY BUTTER

A classic accompaniment to poached or broiled fish, this wonderfully flavored butter is surprisingly good with juicy broiled steak.

Shelf life: 1 week in the refrigerator; 1 month in the freezer

3½oz (100g) anchovy fillets, salted or in oil, soaked in cold water for a few minutes

1 cup (200g) unsalted butter, softened

2–3 tbsp chopped fresh basil or dill

1–2 tbsp lemon juice (optional)

salt, if necessary, and freshly ground black pepper

Either pound the anchovies in a mortar and pestle or purée in a food processor. Add the butter and blend well. Add the basil or dill, the lemon juice, if using, and season to taste. Roll into a sausage shape (see opposite) and chill until firm.

LEMON BUTTER

This is delicious with smoked salmon sandwiches and broiled fish, or to add a subtle lemon flavor to sauces. For lime butter use lime juice and peel instead of lemon.

Shelf life: 1 week in the refrigerator; 1 month in the freezer

1 cup (200g) unsalted butter, softened

4 tbsp lemon juice

grated peel of 1 lemon

1–2 tbsp chopped fresh dill or parsley (optional)

salt and freshly ground black pepper

Place the butter in a bowl and beat with the lemon juice until light and fluffy. Add the rest of the ingredients and mix well. Roll (see opposite) and chill until firm.

GARLIC BUTTER

One of the essential stand-bys of my kitchen; spread it thickly on a baguette for the classic garlic bread, or add to hot stews or soups for a subtle aroma of freshly mashed garlic.

Shelf life: 1 week in the refrigerator; 1 month in the freezer

1 cup (200g) unsalted butter, softened

1 tbsp lemon juice (optional)

4–6 garlic cloves, puréed

2 tbsp finely chopped fresh parsley (optional)

salt and freshly ground black pepper

Place the butter in a bowl and beat with the lemon juice until light and fluffy. Add the garlic and parsley, if using, season to taste, and mix well. Roll into a sausage shape (see opposite) and chill until firm.

RIGHT, FROM TOP TO BOTTOM: ANCHOVY, CHILI, LEMONGRASS & LIME, TOMATO, AND GARLIC BUTTERS

COOKING SAUCES

It is hard to define cooking sauces, even though every cuisine has them – basic sauce-like stews

to which meat, fish, or vegetables are added and cooked. Unlike many modern dishes, these

more hearty sauces can be stretched to feed large numbers if necessary; they are designed to be

eaten with bread, noodles, rice, or other starchy accompaniments for a satisfying meal.

SPICY TOMATO & CHILI SAUCE FOR FISH ▷

This piquant sauce is ideal as a base for fish stew. It can also be poured, hot or cold, over sautéed, broiled, or poached fish.

Enough for 2lb (1kg) fish steaks or fillets

Shelf life: 3 weeks in the refrigerator

See page 15 for illustration

4 tbsp olive oil

2 onions, chopped

6 garlic cloves, minced

6 anchovy fillets

1½lb (750g) plum tomatoes, quartered

1 tart apple, peeled, cored, and chopped

2–3 tbsp tomato paste (optional)

juice and grated peel of 1 lemon

2–3 red chilies, such as red jalapeño, Anaheim, or serrano, (or more to taste) finely chopped

salt, if necessary

1 Heat the oil in a pan; add the onions, garlic, and anchovies and sauté until the onions are translucent and soft.

2 Add the tomatoes and apple and simmer for about 30 minutes or until most of the liquid has evaporated.

3 Transfer to a food processor and process to a smooth sauce.

4 Press through a strainer into a clean pan. Add the tomato paste, if using, lemon juice and peel, and chilies. Bring to a boil and boil for 2–3 minutes. Add salt if necessary (the anchovies are salty).

5 To use, either pour over fish steaks and bake for about 25 minutes or simply serve as an accompaniment to poached, broiled, or sautéed fish.

VARIATIONS

SPICY TOMATO & FENNEL SAUCE
Sauté 1 finely chopped celery heart, 1 finely chopped small fennel bulb, and ½ teaspoon fennel seeds with the onion, garlic, and anchovies in step 1.

SPICY PEPPER SAUCE
Substitute 2lb (1kg) seeded and sliced red peppers for the tomatoes. Omit the apple and the tomato paste.

Opposite: cod fillets in Spicy Tomato & Chili Sauce

DRY CURRY

Dry curries vary in strength and flavor, but all are based on a flavoring paste that is sautéed with the meat until it browns; then a little liquid is added and the meat is cooked until tender. This recipe is especially good made with lamb or beef but also works well with vegetables. For an authentic flavor, use a mortar and pestle to make the spice paste and relish its full aroma. The masala (a spice mix, usually dry-roasted whole, then ground) is also integral to the curry's distinctive flavors.

For the spice paste

3 onions, chopped

6 garlic cloves, peeled

2 inches (5cm) fresh ginger, peeled

2–6 thin green chilies, to taste, seeded

1 tsp turmeric

1 tsp chili powder

For the masala

6 green cardamom pods

6 cloves

2 tsp coriander seeds

1 tsp cumin seeds

2 inches (5cm) cinnamon stick or a few pieces of cassia

For the curry

4 tbsp ghee or oil

1½lb (750g) stewing lamb or beef

3 tbsp yogurt, beaten with 1 cup (250ml) water

8 fresh curry leaves (optional)

chopped cilantro, to serve

1 To make the spice paste, put all the ingredients in a food processor and process to a smooth purée.

2 Make the masala as shown below.

3 Heat the ghee or oil in a large pan; add the spice paste and sauté for 2–3 minutes or until it begins to give off a pleasant aroma. Add the meat, sprinkle with half the masala, and fry, stirring and scraping the base of the pan, for 15–20 minutes or until nicely browned.

4 Reduce the heat, sprinkle with about 3 tablespoons of the diluted yogurt; then cover and simmer very slowly for about 1½–2 hours, adding more yogurt when the mixture becomes dry. If all the yogurt has been used and the meat is still not tender, add a little water as necessary.

5 Five minutes before the meat is ready, stir in the remaining masala and the curry leaves, if using. Sprinkle with cilantro and serve with rice.

Advance preparation: the masala can be stored in an airtight container for up to 3 months; the spice paste keeps for 1 week in the refrigerator and 3 months in the freezer

Shelf life: 1 week in the refrigerator; 3 months in the freezer

DRY-ROASTING SPICES & MAKING MASALA

1 To dry-roast spices, sauté them in a dry skillet over medium heat until they are lightly browned and beginning to give off an appetizing spicy aroma. Be careful not to burn them – they are ready when they start to pop.

2 If you are making a masala or spice mix, set the roasted spices aside to cool; then transfer to a spice or coffee mill or a mortar.

3 Process in the spice or coffee mill or pound to a fine powder with a mortar and pestle.

4 For a finer powder, sift the powder and grind the larger pieces left in the sifter again.

DRY VEGETABLE CURRY

This is a modern adaptation of an Indian classic. Traditionally, cauliflower or cabbage is used, but I prefer a mixture of vegetables such as green beans, baby carrots, small tender squashes, and, best of all, pumpkin or sweet potatoes. You can make this recipe with paneer or tofu, but fry it gently in oil until lightly browned before adding it to the stew.

Advance preparation: the masala can be stored in an airtight container for up to 3 months; the spice paste keeps for 1 week in the refrigerator and 3 months in the freezer

Shelf life: 1 week in the refrigerator; 3 months in the freezer

For the masala

1 tsp coriander seeds

4 black or green cardamom pods

2 inches (5cm) cinnamon stick or 2–3 pieces of cassia

½ tsp fennel seeds

2 tsp nigella seeds

For the curry

4 tbsp ghee or oil

1 tbsp mixed black and white mustard seeds

2 tbsp white poppy seeds

1 recipe Spice Paste (see Dry Curry, opposite)

4 tbsp yogurt, beaten with 1 cup (200ml) water

1lb (500g) mixed vegetables, such as cauliflower, potato, peas, and green beans, steamed, blanched, or sautéed in oil

chopped cilantro, to serve

1 For the masala, dry-roast all the spices except the nigella seeds; then pound or grind them (see opposite). Dry-roast the nigella seeds and stir them into the masala.

2 Heat the ghee or oil in a skillet; add the mustard and poppy seeds and fry for 1–2 minutes until they start to pop. Add the spice paste and heat for 2–3 minutes or until it gives off a pleasant aroma. Sprinkle with half the masala and fry for 15–20 minutes or until browned.

3 Reduce the heat. Sprinkle with about half the diluted yogurt; then cover and simmer very slowly for about 20 minutes, adding more yogurt if the mixture becomes too dry.

4 Add the vegetables, turning them well in the sauce; add the rest of the yogurt and heat through. Stir in the rest of the masala. Sprinkle with cilantro and serve with rice.

ANGLO-INDIAN CURRY

3 tbsp ghee or oil

1lb (500g) onions, chopped

2 garlic cloves, minced (optional)

2 large dessert apples, peeled, cored, and chopped

1–2 tbsp mild curry powder, or to taste

2 bay leaves, crumbled

a small piece of cinnamon stick or cassia

½ cup (100g) raisins, plumped up in a little hot water

2 cups (500ml) Chicken or Vegetable Stock (see pages 28 and 31) or water

salt

This pleasant, mild, and versatile curry was invented in the kitchens of colonial India, where local cooks adapted traditional curries to suit the British palate. This sauce became very popular in Victorian Britain as a way of using up leftover roast, but you can also fry meat until lightly browned and heat it in the sauce until cooked through.

Enough for 1–1½lb (500–750g) meat or vegetables

Advance preparation: the stock can be made in advance

Shelf life: 1 week in the refrigerator; 3 months in the freezer

1 Heat the ghee or oil in a large pan; add the onions and the garlic, if using, and sauté until golden. Stir in the apples, curry powder, bay leaves, and cinnamon or cassia and cook over a high heat, stirring constantly, for about 3 minutes.

2 Add the raisins and the stock or water. Bring to a boil; then reduce the heat and simmer for about 30 minutes or until most of the liquid has been absorbed and the sauce has thickened. Season with salt to taste.

3 To use, either add cooked meat or vegetables and heat through thoroughly, or pour over hot cooked meat.

LAMB KORMA ▷

Rather than a sauce, korma is the name of a technique in which meat or vegetables are braised in a sauce thickened with onions, yogurt, ground nuts, and fragrant spices. After long, slow cooking, the dish is finished with additional yogurt or cream. The superbly intricate flavor of the korma is achieved by the order and timing in which the spices are added to the sauce. Here is a modern version of this northern Indian dish.

Advance preparation:
the masala can be stored in an airtight container for up to 3 months; the spice paste keeps for 1 week in the refrigerator and 3 months in the freezer

Shelf life: 1 week in the refrigerator; 3 months in the freezer

For the spice paste

4 onions, chopped

4 garlic cloves, peeled

2 inches (5cm) fresh ginger, peeled

3–4 red chilies, seeded

½ cup (60g) almonds or cashew nuts, ground

For the masala

6 green cardamom pods

5–6 cloves

1 inch (2.5cm) cinnamon stick

1 tsp coriander seeds

2 bay leaves

For the stew

6 tbsp ghee or oil

1½lb (750g) lean lamb or beef

1 tbsp white poppy seeds, ground (optional)

1 cup (200ml) yogurt, beaten with ⅔ cup (150ml) water

5 tbsp heavy cream or thick yogurt

12 slivered almonds, browned in the oven or in a little oil

2–3 tbsp fresh mint or cilantro

1 To make the spice paste, process all the ingredients together in a food processor until as smooth as possible.

2 Make the masala (see page 78).

3 Heat the ghee or oil in a large pan; add the spice paste and cook for 5–8 minutes or until it gives off a pleasant, spicy aroma. Add the meat and sprinkle with the poppy seeds, if using, and three-quarters of the masala, mixing well.

4 Sauté, stirring frequently and scraping the bottom of the pan, for about 10–15 minutes or until the mixture dries and begins to brown. Reduce the heat; then add 3 tablespoons of the diluted yogurt; cover and cook gently for 20–25 minutes, stirring and scraping frequently. Add more of the diluted yogurt if necessary to prevent sticking.

5 Stir in the rest of the diluted yogurt, bring to a boil; then reduce the heat and simmer for about 1–1½ hours or until the meat is tender and the sauce has reduced and thickened. Skim off any traces of fat floating on the surface. Add the rest of the masala and the cream or yogurt and boil rapidly for 2 minutes, until the sauce is smooth.

6 Sprinkle with the almonds and mint or cilantro and serve.

VARIATIONS

CHICKEN KORMA
Make a masala with 2 teaspoons coriander seeds, 1 teaspoon cumin seeds, 1 inch (2.5cm) cinnamon stick or cassia, 1 teaspoon fennel seeds, ½ teaspoon mace, and 1 teaspoon sweet or hot paprika; then follow the recipe above, replacing the lamb or beef with 4 boneless, skinless chicken breast halves. Dissolve ¼ teaspoon saffron in a few tablespoons of warm milk or water and stir into the sauce with the chicken.

PANEER OR TOFU KORMA
Korma can easily be adapted for vegetarians. Simply replace the meat with 1½lb (750g) paneer or tofu, drained on paper towels and cut into cubes.
• Sauté the paneer or tofu in 3 tablespoons of the ghee or oil in a pan until golden on all sides. Drain on paper towels and set aside.
• Add the rest of the oil, the spice paste, poppy seeds, and three quarters of the masala and cook until the spice paste starts to brown. Stir in 4–5 tablespoons of the diluted yogurt and bring to a boil. Reduce the heat and simmer for 10 minutes, stirring and scraping the bottom of the pan; then add the rest of the yogurt mixture and bring to a boil. Lower the heat and simmer for about 25 minutes, uncovered, until the sauce has reduced and thickened.
• Add the paneer or tofu, the heavy cream or yogurt, and the rest of the masala and simmer for 5–8 minutes until heated through. Sprinkle with the almonds and herbs before serving.

OPPOSITE: STEPS 3, 4, 5, AND 6 OF MAKING LAMB KORMA

ROGAN JOSH

3 tbsp oil or ghee
6 cloves
2 inches (5cm) cinnamon stick, broken, or 2 pieces of cassia
2–4 small dried red chilies, such as bird's eye, seeded and chopped
2 bay leaves, crumbled
3 onions, grated or finely chopped
4 garlic cloves, crushed
1 inch (2.5cm) fresh ginger, finely shredded
1lb (500g) lamb or beef, cut into 1 inch (2.5cm) cubes
4 tbsp yogurt, mixed with 1¼ cups (300ml) water or stock
1–2 tsp masala (see Lamb Korma, page 80)
2–3 tbsp chopped cilantro

Josh are a vast family of juicy curries in which the aromatics are not pulverized into a paste but used whole. A little masala is added toward the end of cooking for a fresher flavor. Serve this delicious dish with cinnamon-flavored rice or, as I like to eat it, with warm naan or pita bread.

Advance preparation: *the masala can be stored in an airtight container for up to 3 months; the fried spice paste keeps for 1 week in the refrigerator and 3 months in the freezer*

Shelf life: *1 week in the refrigerator; 3 months in the freezer*

1 Heat the oil or ghee in a large pan; add the cloves and sauté for 2 minutes. Stir in the cinnamon or cassia, chilies, and bay leaves and fry for 2–3 minutes or until the bay starts to color. Add the onions, garlic, and ginger and cook for 15–20 minutes or until the onions are golden brown.

2 Add the meat and fry for about 15 minutes or until nicely brown. If the mixture gets too dry, add a few tablespoons of the diluted yogurt.

3 Add the remaining yogurt; bring to a boil. Reduce the heat and simmer very slowly for about 1–1½ hours or until the meat is tender and the sauce has reduced and thickened. Skim any traces of fat from the surface; then stir in the masala and cilantro and serve.

VARIATIONS

TOMATO JOSH
Replace the yogurt with ¾lb (375g) tomatoes, peeled, seeded (see page 43), and chopped, and 2 tablespoons tomato paste.

METHI JOSH
Add 5oz (150g) very finely chopped fresh fenugreek with the onions, garlic, and ginger in step 1.

VANILLA CURRY

For the spice paste
1 large onion, chopped
3 garlic cloves, peeled
1 inch (2.5cm) fresh ginger, peeled
2–3 long, thin red chilies, seeded
For the stew
3 tbsp oil or ghee
1 vanilla pod, finely chopped
4 tbsp yogurt, mixed with 1¼ cups (300ml) coconut milk or water
1 medium pineapple, peeled, cored, and finely chopped
3–4 tbsp chopped cilantro or dill
salt

1 Put all the spice paste ingredients in a food processor and process until smooth.

2 Heat the oil or ghee in a large pan, add half the vanilla and cook for 1–2 minutes or until it starts to give off a pleasant aroma. Add the spice paste and cook for about 10 minutes, stirring and scraping the base of the pan, until evenly golden brown. If the mixture is too dry, add 1–2 spoonfuls of the yogurt mixture.

3 Add the pineapple and sauté for about 5 minutes or until it starts to soften. Add the yogurt mixture; bring to a boil. Turn down the heat and simmer very slowly for about 45 minutes, until the sauce has reduced and thickened. Stir in the cilantro or dill and season with salt to taste.

4 To use, pour the sauce over duck or chicken pieces that have been browned and simmer for 1–1½ hours, until tender. Alternatively, the sauce can be poured over broiled or barbecued poultry.

This is probably my favorite recipe in the book – it is delicately flavored, well balanced, and has a delightfully subtle aroma of vanilla. It is superb with duck and also goes well with free-range chicken or game birds. Since I created this curry, I have tried making it with peach and mango instead of pineapple – both with excellent results. For a stronger vanilla flavor, I sometimes sprinkle the dish with a little finely chopped vanilla bean just before serving.

Enough for about 1–1½lb (500–750g) boneless duck or chicken brests

Advance preparation: *the cooked spice paste (without the coconut milk) keeps for 2 weeks in the refrigerator and 3 months in the freezer*

Shelf life: *1 week in the refrigerator; 3 months in the freezer*

SABZI

In Iran, brides were judged on their ability to prepare this superbly delicate dish. Minutely chopping the enormous quantity of herbs required a great deal of skill – rendered particularly arduous under the watchful eye of the mother-in-law. These days, the herbs are chopped in a food processor or in a specially designed mill. Dried limes, or lamoo, are a popular flavoring in Iranian food and are available in Middle Eastern and Indian foodstores – if you can't find them, omit them altogether. Serve with plain boiled rice or a rice or bulgur pilaf.

Advance preparation:
the cooked herb mixture keeps for 2 weeks in the refrigerator and 3 months in the freezer

Shelf life: *1 week in the refrigerator; 3 months in the freezer*

1 small (250g) leek
7 cups (100g) fresh flat-leaf parsley (leaves only)
7 cups (100g) cilantro (leaves and stalks)
¼lb (100g) green tops of fresh garlic or garlic chives (optional)
5½ cups (100g) fresh dill, stems removed
6 cups (100g) fresh mint (leaves only)
1¾oz (50g) fresh fenugreek, hard stems removed
½ cup (125ml) sesame or olive oil
⅔ cup (100g) dried kidney beans, soaked in cold water overnight, then drained
3 onions, chopped
1½lb (750g) shoulder or leg of lamb, cut into large chunks
Chicken Stock (see page 28) or water to cover
4 dried limes, rinsed in boiling water and pierced in several places with the point of a sharp knife
2 tbsp lime juice
salt

1 Wash and dry the leek and the herbs; then chop finely by hand or in a food processor. Heat about three-quarters of the oil in a large, heavy skillet and add the leek and herbs. Sauté over medium heat, turning the mixture constantly, for 20–25 minutes or until it darkens. If it seems too dry, add a little water. Put the kidney beans in a separate pan; cover with water and bring to a hard boil for 10 minutes. Drain well.

2 Heat the remaining oil in a deep pan and cook the onions until golden. Add the meat and fry until brown. Add the herb mixture, the beans, and enough stock or water to cover. Bring to a boil; then reduce the heat, cover, and simmer gently for 45 minutes.

3 Add the limes and some salt; simmer for 45–60 minutes or until the meat is tender and the sauce has thickened. Stir in the lime juice and season with salt.

PLUM SAUCE FOR FISH

3 tbsp sesame or peanut oil
a small piece of stick cinnamon, crumbled
1–2 dried bird's eye chilies
½ cup (100g) shallots, chopped
5 garlic cloves, minced
1 inch (2.5cm) fresh ginger, finely chopped or grated
2 cups (300g) plums, pitted and coarsely chopped
1¼ cups (300ml) Fish Stock (see page 30), rice wine, or dry white wine
1 tbsp dark soy sauce
1–1½ tbsp sugar
2 star anise
½ tsp ground Szechwan pepper
salt

1 Heat the oil in a wok or a large frying pan; add the cinnamon and chilies and fry over high heat for 2–3 minutes or until the cinnamon gives off a pleasant aroma and the chilies are browned. Lift out and discard. Add the shallots, garlic, and ginger and sauté for 5 minutes or until the shallots soften and start to color.

2 Add all the remaining ingredients and bring to a boil. Reduce the heat and simmer for about 30 minutes or until the sauce has thickened and reduced.

3 Either use the sauce as is or purée in a blender and strain it for a smooth texture.

4 To use, either pour over raw fish and bake until the fish is done, or bring to a boil and pour over baked or steamed fish; allow the fish to absorb the flavor for a few minutes; then serve.

A fragrant, delicate sauce that goes well with freshwater fish such as carp, trout, or tilapia but is also delicious with fatty ocean fish such as mackerel or sardines.

Enough for 1lb (500g) fish

Advance preparation:
the fish stock can be made in advance

Shelf life: 1 week in the refrigerator; 3 months in the freezer

SWEET & SOUR SAUCE

This sauce is rumored to have been invented by Chinese cooks in the railroad canteens of the Wild West. It became one of the most used and abused of Chinese sauces. Made properly, sweet and sour sauce is delicious and versatile. Serve it with chicken, fish, or pork, or as a dip or side sauce.

Enough for 1½lb (750g) chicken, fish, or pork

Shelf life: *2 weeks in the refrigerator; 3 months in the freezer*

3 tbsp peanut or sesame oil
4 garlic cloves, finely minced
1 inch (2.5cm) fresh ginger, finely shredded
1 carrot, finely shredded
1–2 hot red chilies such as Thai or bird's eye, seeded and minced (optional)
⅔ cup (150ml) water
⅔ cup (150ml) rice vinegar
⅔ cup (150ml) tomato ketchup
4–5 tbsp honey or sugar
1–2 tbsp cornstarch dissolved in 2 tbsp water

1 Heat the oil in a wok or a large skillet; add the garlic, ginger, carrot, and chilies, if using, and sauté for a few minutes until softened. Add all the remaining ingredients except the cornstarch. Bring to a boil, then reduce the heat and simmer for 5 minutes.

2 Add the cornstarch and simmer for a few minutes or until the sauce has thickened.

3 To use, bring to a boil, pour over hot fried or broiled food and serve immediately.

VARIATION

FRUITY SWEET & SOUR SAUCE
Replace the water with pineapple, peach, passion fruit, or apricot juice and, in the final stages of cooking, add about ⅓ cup (75g) of the corresponding finely chopped fresh fruit. Omit the honey or sugar. You could also use canned fruit and a little of the syrup to taste.

BLACK BEAN SAUCE

4 tbsp peanut or sesame oil
2 garlic cloves, minced
½ inch (1cm) fresh ginger, shredded
1–2 red or green chilies, seeded and chopped
3 tbsp fermented black beans, soaked in cold water for 20 minutes, then drained and coarsely chopped
1 tsp rice flour or cornstarch
1½ cups (350ml) Chicken Stock (see page 28)
1 tbsp sweet soy sauce or 1 tbsp dark soy sauce and 2 tsp dark brown sugar
2 tbsp rice wine or sherry
1–2 tsp dark sesame oil

You either like or dislike the flavor of fermented and salted black beans. Here they are used to make one of China's most classic sauces. I also use them instead of salt in meat and vegetable stews. Salted black beans can be bought in Chinese food stores.

Enough for 1lb (500g) chicken, lamb, beef, or seafood and 2lb (1kg) mussels

Shelf life: *2 weeks in the refrigerator; 3 months in the freezer*

1 Heat the oil in a wok or a large skillet. Add the garlic, ginger, and chilies and stir-fry for 1 minute. Add the black beans and stir-fry for 1–2 minutes or until the garlic starts to change color.

2 Dissolve the rice flour or cornstarch in 1 tablespoon of the chicken stock and add to the pan with the remaining stock and all the rest of the ingredients. Bring to a boil, stirring constantly, and cook for 1–2 minutes or until thickened.

3 To use, add to beef, lamb, chicken, or fish in the final stages of stir-frying, or use to steam mussels or other seafood.

RED CURRY PASTE

A wonderful hot, sweet, and fragrant adaptation of a Southeast Asian classic. Other fruit, such as papaya, mango, or banana, can be substituted for the pineapple.

Enough for about 1–1½lb (500–750g) fish or meat

Shelf life: 1 week in the refrigerator; 6 months in a sealed jar (see pages 134–35)

1 large onion, coarsely chopped
6 garlic cloves, peeled
1 small pineapple, peeled, cored, and coarsely chopped
4–6 large red chilies, to taste
2 inches (5cm) fresh ginger or galangal, coarsely chopped
6 tbsp peanut or sesame oil
2 tbsp sugar
3 tbsp Thai fish sauce (*nam pla*)
⅓ cup (100ml) coconut milk

1 Place the onion, garlic, pineapple, chilies, and ginger or galangal in a baking pan, sprinkle with the oil and sugar and mix well. Place in an oven preheated to 375°F/190°C and bake, turning the ingredients and basting with the pan juices occasionally, for about 1 hour or until evenly browned.

2 Allow to cool slightly, then process to a smooth purée in a food processor or blender. Transfer the purée to a clean pan; add the fish sauce and coconut milk. Bring to a boil and cook, stirring constantly, for 3–4 minutes or until the sauce has thickened and most of the liquid has evaporated.

3 To use, put 4–6 tablespoons of the paste and 1¾ cups (400ml) coconut milk in a pan with cubed meat or fish and simmer until cooked. The paste can also be rubbed on raw meat and left to marinate for 2–3 hours before roasting.

YELLOW CURRY PASTE

For the spice paste
⅔ cup (150g) red shallots or onions, chopped
4 garlic cloves, peeled
3 lemongrass stalks, hard outer layers removed, chopped
1–3 yellow or green chilies, to taste, such as green bird's eye, seeded
½ inch (1cm) fresh galangal or ginger
3 tbsp Thai fish sauce (*nam pla*)
For the curry
4 tbsp sesame or peanut oil
½ tsp turmeric
4 tbsp yellow bean paste
2½oz (75g) tamarind pulp, soaked in 1 cup (200ml) hot water, then strained (see page 124)
1 tsp palm sugar or brown sugar
1¾ cups (400ml) coconut milk
⅓ cup (100ml) water
5 tbsp chopped basil

1 For the spice paste, place all the ingredients in a blender or food processor and process to a smooth purée. If too dry add 1–2 tablespoons of water.

2 Heat the oil in a wok or frying pan; add the turmeric and fry for 1 minute. Add the spice paste and fry for 8–10 minutes, until it is fragrant and starting to brown.

3 Add the yellow bean paste, tamarind water, and sugar and mix well, mashing and mixing the paste into the liquid. Bring to a boil; then reduce the heat and simmer for 15 minutes or until thickened. Add the coconut milk and water and boil for 2–3 minutes.

4 To use: pour over fish steaks that have been dusted with cornstarch and lightly browned in oil. Simmer for 8–10 minutes, until the fish is done; then serve sprinkled with the chopped basil.

Yellow bean paste is somewhat an acquired taste. Strongly aromatic, it is made from unsalted, fermented soy beans. Like Japanese miso, it is used to flavor and thicken sauces, stews, and soups. Yellow bean paste is available in jars or cans at most Chinese and Southeast Asian food stores.

Enough for about 1–1½lb (500–750g) fish

Advance preparation: the cooked spice paste keeps for 1 week in the refrigerator and 3 months in the freezer

Shelf life: 1 week in the refrigerator; 3 months in the freezer

LIGHT CURRY FOR FISH

Here is a Thai-style curry that is best served over rice noodles. It is delicious with any firm-fleshed fish, cut into cubes, or a combination of seafood such as shrimp and scallops. You can also cook steamed vegetables, tofu, or paneer in this sauce. If using tofu or paneer, brown it first in a little oil before adding it to the curry in the final cooking stages.

Enough for 1–1½lb (500–750g) fish

Advance preparation: the cooked spice paste (without the coconut milk) keeps for 2 weeks in the refrigerator and 3 months in the freezer

Shelf life: 1 week in the refrigerator; 3 months in the freezer

3 tbsp peanut, sunflower, or sesame oil
2 (125g) carrots, cut into fine julienne
2–6 hot green or red chilies, to taste, seeded and finely sliced
14 (200g) shallots or 1 onion, finely sliced
5 large garlic cloves, finely shredded
1 inch (2.5cm) fresh ginger, finely shredded
2 lemongrass stalks, hard outer layers removed, finely chopped
½ tsp turmeric
4–5 kaffir lime leaves, shredded
1 cup (250ml) Fish Stock (see page 30)
1¾ cups (400ml) coconut milk
juice of 1 lime and grated peel of ½ lime
2–3 tbsp Thai fish sauce (*nam pla*) or salt to taste
3 tbsp chopped fresh basil or cilantro

1 Heat the oil in a large wok or skillet. Add the carrots and chilies and stir-fry for 2–3 minutes. Add the shallots, garlic, ginger, and lemongrass and stir-fry until all are evenly golden. Add the turmeric and half the kaffir lime leaves and cook for a further 1–2 minutes.

2 Pour in the stock and coconut milk and bring to a boil; then reduce the heat and simmer gently for about 20 minutes or until the liquid has reduced by one fourth and has thickened slightly. Add the lime juice and peel and the fish sauce or salt and stir well.

3 To use, add cubed fish or other seafood to the sauce and cook for 5–8 minutes or until the fish is done. Stir in the remaining kaffir lime leaves and the basil or cilantro and serve.

GREEN CURRY PASTE ▷

16 (250g) shallots, unpeeled
1 large head of garlic, unpeeled
4–6 green chilies, to taste
1 inch (2.5cm) fresh galangal or ginger, chopped
5 lemongrass stalks, hard outer layers removed, chopped
1 large bunch of cilantro (roots, stalks, and leaves), coarsely chopped
3–4 tbsp Thai fish sauce (*nam pla*)
1–2 tbsp palm sugar or brown sugar
4 tbsp peanut or sesame oil

1 Place the shallots and garlic on a baking tray and bake in an oven preheated to 425°F/220°C for 20–25 minutes or until lightly browned and easily pierced with a knife. Let them cool.

2 Peel the shallots and squeeze the garlic out of its skin.

3 Place the chilies in a pan with just enough water to cover, bring to a boil, and simmer for about 10 minutes or until soft. Cool under cold water, then seed and coarsely chop.

4 Place the shallots, garlic, chilies, and all the remaining ingredients except the oil in a blender (for a smooth paste) or food processor (for a coarser texture) and process. If too dry, add a little water.

5 Heat the oil in a wok or skillet; add the paste and fry for 5–8 minutes or until most of the liquid has evaporated and the paste has darkened slightly. Let it cool. The paste can be transferred to sterilized jars, if desired.

6 To use, dilute 12–18 tablespoons (2–3 tablespoons per person) of paste in a pan with 1¾ cups (400ml) coconut milk and bring to a boil. Add shrimp or other seafood. Reduce the heat and simmer for 10 minutes. If the sauce is too thin, take out the seafood and boil the sauce until it thickens.

This popular Thai curry paste is normally prepared in large quantities and used as a base for hot and refreshing shrimp or seafood curries, to finish soups and stews, and to add instant flavor to many dishes. Traditionally, the recipe includes shrimp paste, an aromatic purée made from fermented shrimp and fish, but you can use fish sauce or anchovy paste instead.

Enough for 1lb (500g) shrimp or other seafood

Shelf life: 2 weeks refrigerated in a tightly sealed jar (make sure there is a protective layer of oil over the paste); 3 months in the freezer; 6 months in a sealed jar (see pages 134–35)

OPPOSITE: STEPS 1, 2, 4, AND 5 OF MAKING GREEN CURRY PASTE

MOLE

Mole is one of the signature sauces of Mexican cuisine. The story goes that it was invented by Spanish nuns in the 18th century, but, in fact, refried pastes of dried chilies combined with purées of fruit, spices, herbs, and chocolate had been used by the indigenous population for centuries. Making traditional mole is a very complex process, and recipes vary from region to region and even from family to family. This recipe is a simplified version and gives a thick, flavorsome, medium-hot sauce. Mexican ingredients are available in many large supermarkets and specialty stores. The dried chilies give mole its characteristic slightly bitter flavor. Traditionally, the sauce is poured over poached turkey, chicken, or pork, and the cooking liquid is used instead of stock. Serve with lots of soft tortillas to mop up the delicious sauce.

For the paste

2 each of the following dried chilies: ancho, guajillo, pasilla, and mulato, hard stems removed and seeded

1 dried chipotle chili, seeded

1 onion, unpeeled

1 head of garlic, unpeeled

4 plum tomatoes

2 tortillas or 1 thick slice of white bread, cut into chunks

1 ripe plantain or banana, peeled

For the spice mix

5–6 allspice berries

2–3 cloves

1 inch (2.5cm) cinnamon stick or cassia, crumbled

For the mole

4 tbsp olive oil

½ cup (75g) raisins, plumped in a little boiling water for 20 minutes

¼ cup (30g) blanched almonds, browned in a little oil, then ground

2 tbsp (30g) sesame or pumpkin seeds, browned in a little oil, then ground (reserve some whole seeds for garnish)

1 tsp dried oregano

1 tsp dried thyme

1³⁄₄oz (50g) unsweetened, dark chocolate or 2 tbsp unsweetened cocoa

2½ cups (600ml) Chicken Stock (see page 28)

salt

1 For the paste, place the chilies, onion, garlic, tomatoes, and tortillas or bread on a well-greased baking sheet and roast in an oven preheated to 425°F/220°C.

Remove the chilies after about 2–3 minutes; they should be fragrant and beginning to change color. Place them in a bowl; cover with boiling water and let them soak for 30 minutes.

2 Remove the tortillas or bread when lightly browned, but continue to roast the onion, garlic, and tomatoes until soft, a further 20 minutes or so.

3 Drain the chilies. Taste the soaking liquid and, if it's not too bitter, reserve it. Purée the chilies in a blender or food processor. Add the plantain or banana and the roasted ingredients and process to a smooth paste. If too dry, add a few tablespoons of water, stock, or the chilli soaking liquid.

4 Dry-roast and grind the spice mix (see page 78).

5 Heat the oil in a large pan; add the paste, the spice mix, and all the remaining ingredients except the chocolate or cocoa, the stock, and the salt. Cook for 8–10 minutes over medium heat, stirring constantly and scraping the bottom of the pan until most of the liquid has evaporated.

6 Add the chocolate or cocoa and stir until melted and well blended. Stir in the stock, bring to a boil, and simmer for about 8–10 minutes or until the sauce coats the back of a spoon. Add salt to taste and garnish with the reserved sesame or pumpkin seeds.

7 To use, pour over poached or roast turkey, chicken, or pork and heat through before serving.

Advance preparation: the spice paste keeps for 1 week in the refrigerator and 3 months in the freezer

Shelf life: 1 week in the refrigerator; 3 months in the freezer

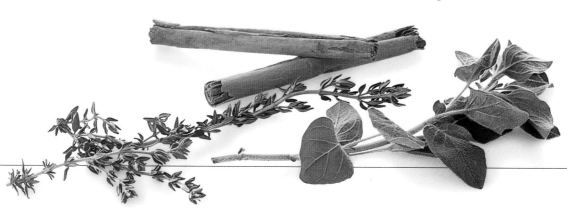

CHILI CON CARNE

This internationally renowned dish was invented by Mexican farm workers in the wilds of southwestern America in the middle of the 19th century. Flavored with chili, cumin, and tomatoes, it is a substantial meal in itself, with all the fire of Mexican food. Mixed with generous amounts of melted Monterey Jack or Cheddar cheese, it can be served as a dip with tortillas or as a filling for enchiladas and soft tortillas. It goes with hamburgers and, of course, rice.

Serves 8–10

Shelf life: 1 week in the refrigerator; 3 months in the freezer

4–6 dried red chilies, such as ancho or New Mexico red, hard stems removed and seeded, or chili powder to taste
4 tbsp olive oil
½–1 tsp cumin seeds
2 onions, chopped
8 large garlic cloves, finely chopped
2–3 tsp dried oregano
1½lb (750g) lean ground beef
1 x 14oz (200g) cans of tomatoes
2–3 generous tbsp tomato paste
2 x 15oz (400g) cans of red kidney beans, or 1⅔ cups (250g) dried kidney beans, cooked
chili powder to taste
5 tbsp chopped cilantro
salt

1 Place the chilies in a small pan; pour boiling water over them to cover and simmer until the skins begin to split and the chilies are soft, about 20 minutes. Drain, reserving about ⅔ cup (150ml) of the water if it is not too bitter. Transfer the chilies to a blender or food processor and process to a smooth purée with either the reserved water or fresh water if that is too bitter.

2 Heat the oil in a heavy pan; add the cumin seeds, onions, garlic, and oregano and sauté until the onions start to brown. Add the meat and stir well to break it up. Reduce the heat, cover, and cook for about 15–20 minutes, stirring frequently, until the meat is tender and most of the liquid has evaporated.

3 Add the tomatoes with the juices, the chili purée, and the tomato paste and bring to a boil. Reduce the heat and simmer, partially covered, for about 30 minutes, stirring frequently. Add the kidney beans and salt to taste and continue cooking for 30–45 minutes, or until the sauce has reduced and thickened. Taste the chili and add some chili powder, if desired. Sprinkle with the cilantro and serve.

MANCHAMANTEL

3 dried ancho chilies, seeded
2 dried mulato chilies, seeded
6 tbsp olive oil
1 small onion, coarsely chopped
4 garlic cloves, minced
3 ripe bananas, coarsely chopped
1lb (500g) plum tomatoes, peeled and seeded (see page 43)
2 tsp ground cinnamon
¼ tsp ground cloves
¼ tsp ground allspice
2 tbsp dried oregano
salt

1 Place the chilies on a baking sheet and roast in an oven preheated to 425°F/220°C for 2–3 minutes, until fragrant. Transfer the chilies to a bowl, cover with boiling water, and let them soak for 30 minutes. Drain well, reserving the soaking liquid if it is not too bitter.

2 Heat 4 tablespoons of the olive oil in a frying pan; add the onion, garlic, and bananas and fry for 10–15 minutes, until nicely browned.

3 Put the banana mixture, chilies, and tomatoes in a blender or food processor and process to a smooth purée. Add a little of the chili soaking liquid or water to the processor if the mixture is too dry.

4 Heat the remaining oil in a deep skillet and add the cinnamon, cloves, allspice, and oregano. Add the purée and cook, stirring occasionally, for 5–8 minutes or until the sauce has thickened and most of the liquid has evaporated. Season with salt to taste.

5 To use: add cubed and browned beef or lamb to the sauce and simmer until tender. Add a few tablespoons of water while cooking if it becomes too dry.

Sweet, hot, and intense in flavor, this dark-red sauce originates in central Mexico, where its name literally means tablecloth stainer. It can be made from fruit other than bananas, such as pineapple, mango, or papaya.

Enough for about 1–1½lb (500–750g) beef or lamb

Shelf life: 3 weeks in the refrigerator; 3 months in the freezer

PASTA SAUCES

THESE QUICK, DELICIOUS, and healthy sauces are popular with many busy cooks because they are so easy to make. Some of them are classics, but I have also included modern variations of the old favorites. What they all have in common is their freshness and the use of readily available, seasonal ingredients.

PASSATA

A versatile tomato sauce that can be used as a base for many dishes. I make it in large quantities if garden-ripe tomatoes are available because it can be frozen or preserved very successfully. For a spicier version, add fresh or dried chili to taste. If you prefer a smooth sauce, don't peel the tomatoes – simply strain the finished sauce. Add a little sugar if the tomatoes are too tart.

Makes 1½ quarts (1.5 liters)

Shelf life: 1 week in the refrigerator; 3 months in the freezer; 6 months in a sealed jar (see pages 134–35)

½ cup (125ml) olive oil

1lb (500g) onions, chopped

6 garlic cloves, minced

4lb (2kg) plum tomatoes, peeled, seeded (see page 43), and chopped

a bouquet garni made with a few sprigs of parsley and oregano, a few celery leaves, a bay leaf and 1 strip of lemon peel (optional) (see page 30)

2 tsp sugar (optional)

salt and freshly ground black pepper

Heat the oil in a large pan; add the onions and garlic and sauté over medium heat until the onions are translucent. Add the tomatoes and the bouquet garni, if using, and simmer for about 1 hour, or until most of the liquid has evaporated. Remove the bouquet garni; then taste the sauce and add sugar, if necessary, and salt and pepper.

ARRABBIATA

6 tbsp olive oil

1–3 tsp dried chili flakes, to taste

4 garlic cloves, minced

1lb (500g) plum tomatoes, peeled, seeded (see page 43), and chopped

1 tsp sugar (optional)

3 tbsp chopped fresh flat-leaf parsley

salt

Heat the oil in a large skillet; add the chili flakes and garlic and sauté for 4–5 minutes, or until the garlic starts to turn golden. Add the tomatoes and simmer, stirring from time to time, until they have begun to disintegrate and the sauce has thickened, about 15 minutes. Taste the sauce and add sugar if necessary, then stir in the parsley and season to taste with salt.

This spicy tomato sauce can be served on pasta (traditionally penne) or poured over freshly broiled steaks, chops, or broiled or roasted vegetables.

Shelf life: 1 week in the refrigerator; 3 months in the freezer; 6 months in a sealed jar (see pages 134–35)

EGGPLANT SAUCE

Eggplants make a delicious, versatile sauce that can be served with pasta, noodles, and rice or other cooked grains. I sometimes add 2 tablespoons of soy sauce, which gives an extra flavor dimension.

Advance preparation: the passata can be made in advance

Shelf life: 1 week in the refrigerator; 3 months in the freezer

2 tsp salt

1 small or ½ large (250g) eggplant, cut into ½ inch (1cm) cubes

3 tbsp olive oil

1 large onion, chopped

4 garlic cloves, minced

2 tbsp dark soy sauce

⅔ cup (150ml) Passata (see above) or 3 tbsp tomato paste diluted with ½ cup (100ml) water

3–4 (250g) plum tomatoes, peeled, seeded (see page 43), and chopped

3 tbsp chopped fresh thyme or oregano

salt and freshly ground black pepper

1 Sprinkle the salt over the eggplant in a colander and set aside to drain for about 30 minutes. Pat dry with paper towels.

2 Heat the oil in a large skillet; add the onion and garlic and sauté until the onion starts to color, about 5–8 minutes. Add the eggplant and sauté until it softens a little. Add the soy sauce and cook until it is absorbed; then add the passata or the diluted tomato paste. Cover the sauce and simmer until the eggplant is very soft, about 10 minutes.

3 Stir in the tomatoes and thyme or oregano; heat through and season to taste with salt and freshly ground black pepper.

TOMATO & TUNA SAUCE

A Mediterranean pasta sauce that is robust in flavor and very easy to prepare.

Shelf life: *1 week in the refrigerator; 3 months in the freezer; 6 months in a sealed jar (see pages 134–35)*

4 tbsp olive oil
1 tsp fennel seeds (optional)
1 large onion, chopped
3 garlic cloves, minced
4 anchovy fillets, chopped
1lb (500g) plum tomatoes, peeled, seeded (see page 43), and chopped
2 tbsp tomato paste, diluted in ⅓ cup (100ml) red or white wine, stock, or water
a bouquet garni made with a few sprigs of thyme, fennel leaves, parsley, and 2 strips of lemon peel (see page 30)
7oz (200g) can of tuna, packed in water or oil, drained and crumbled
2 tbsp capers, rinsed and coarsely chopped (left whole if small)
3 tbsp chopped fresh flat-leaf parsley or 2 tbsp chopped fresh lemon thyme or tarragon
salt, if necessary, and freshly ground black pepper

1 Heat the oil in a large skillet; add the fennel seeds, if using, and cook for 2–3 minutes or until they begin to give off a pleasant spicy aroma. Stir in the onion and garlic and sauté until the onion has started to color, about 5 minutes. Add the anchovies and stir until they start to break up.

2 Add the tomatoes, the diluted tomato paste, and the bouquet garni; bring to a boil. Reduce the heat and simmer until most of the liquid has evaporated, about 30 minutes.

3 Stir in the tuna, capers, and parsley, lemon thyme, or tarragon. Season to taste and simmer for a further 2–3 minutes.

TOMATO & BROILED ZUCCHINI SAUCE

2 tsp salt
½lb (250g) zucchini, cut into slices ¾ inch (2cm) thick
6 tbsp olive oil
10 (150g) shallots, quartered
6 garlic cloves, quartered
1lb (500g) plum tomatoes, peeled, seeded (see page 43), and chopped
2 tbsp canned tomato paste, diluted in ⅓ cup (100ml) red or white wine, stock, or water
a bouquet garni made with a few sprigs of thyme, rosemary, parsley, and 2 strips of orange peel (see page 30)
2 tbsp chopped fresh thyme or 3 tbsp chopped fresh flat-leaf parsley
salt and freshly ground black pepper

Roasting or broiling the zucchini keeps them fresh and crunchy. Pour this sauce over tagliatelle, pappardelle, or any other flat ribbon pasta and serve with plenty of grated Parmesan.

Shelf life: *1 week in the refrigerator; 3 months in the freezer; 6 months in a sealed jar (see pages 134–35)*

1 Sprinkle the salt over the zucchini in a colander and set aside to drain for 30 minutes. Pat dry with paper towels.

2 Heat 4 tablespoons of the oil in a large skillet; add the shallots and garlic and sauté until golden, about 7–8 minutes. Add the tomatoes, the diluted tomato paste, and the bouquet garni and bring to a boil. Reduce the heat and simmer for about 30 minutes or until most of the liquid has evaporated.

3 Brush the zucchini slices with the remaining oil and cook under a hot broiler, turning until browned on both sides. Add to the sauce along with the thyme or parsley and salt and pepper. Simmer for 3–4 minutes.

VONGOLE

My friend Brad gave me this recipe – it is the easiest and most effective way to make this Italian classic. It differs slightly from the traditional vongole in that the tomatoes are just heated through rather than cooked.

Shelf life: *1 week in the refrigerator*

6–8 tbsp extra virgin olive oil

1–2 tbsp dried chili flakes

4 garlic cloves, minced

9oz (290g) canned clams, drained

4 (250g) plum tomatoes, peeled, seeded (see page 43), and finely chopped

a small bunch of fresh flat-leaf parsley or basil, roughly torn

salt and freshly ground black pepper

Heat the oil in a large skillet; add the chili and sauté over a high heat for 2–3 minutes. Add the garlic and cook until it starts to color. Stir in the clams, turning them in the oil to heat through; then add the tomatoes and stir until the sauce is hot. Season to taste and stir in the herbs.

THREE-TOMATO SAUCE

This pasta sauce is also delicious served with broiled, fried, or barbecued chicken. Sun-dried tomatoes in oil are not suitable for this recipe; use the loose dried variety instead.

Advance preparation: *the passata can be made in advance*

Shelf life: *1 week in the refrigerator; 3 months in the freezer; 6 months in a sealed jar (see pages 134–35)*

4 tbsp olive oil

4 garlic cloves, thinly sliced

2 cups (500ml) Passata (see page 90)

1 cup (250ml) red wine

3½oz (100g) sun-dried tomatoes, soaked in hot water for 20 minutes, then drained and sliced into fine julienne

½lb (250g) cherry or small plum tomatoes

a small bunch of fresh basil, torn

salt and freshly ground black pepper

1 Heat the oil in a large skillet; add the garlic and sauté until it turns golden. Add the passata, wine, and sun-dried tomatoes and bring to a boil; then reduce the heat and simmer until reduced by a third, about 20 minutes.

2 Roast the cherry or plum tomatoes in a very hot oven or in a dry skillet until lightly charred and soft. Fold them into the sauce with the basil; then season to taste with salt and freshly ground pepper.

WILD MUSHROOM SAUCE

3 tbsp olive oil

1 large onion, chopped

2 garlic cloves, minced

½lb (250g) shiitake mushrooms, stems removed, sliced

½lb (250g) oyster mushrooms, torn into pieces

½oz (15g) dried porcini, soaked in ⅓ cup (75ml) hot water for 20 minutes, drained, soaking liquid reserved

1 tbsp dark soy sauce

1½ cups (350ml) Chicken or Vegetable Stock (see pages 28 and 31)

⅔ cup (150ml) white wine

2 tbsp chopped fresh thyme or oregano

5 tbsp (75g) butter, chilled and cubed (optional)

salt and freshly ground black pepper

A real favorite of mine, this pasta sauce is quite a luxury. Experiment with different varieties of mushroom depending on what is available.

Advance preparation: *the stock can be made in advance*

Shelf life: *1 week in the refrigerator*

1 Heat the oil in a large skillet; add the onion and garlic and sauté until golden. Add all the mushrooms, including the porcini, and the soy sauce and cook until the mushrooms are limp.

2 Strain the porcini soaking liquid and add to the pan with the stock and wine. Simmer for about 30 minutes, or until most of the liquid has evaporated and the sauce has thickened.

3 Add the thyme or oregano and, if an extra-rich flavor is desired, beat in the butter a little at a time. Season to taste.

VARIATION

CREAMY MUSHROOM SAUCE
Substitute ¾lb (350g) finely sliced button mushrooms for the wild mushrooms and omit the soy sauce. Use ⅔ cup (150ml) chicken or vegetable stock or white wine instead of the 1½ cups (350ml) chicken stock and ⅔ cup (150ml) white wine. Simmer for about 15 minutes; then stir in 1 cup (250ml) heavy cream or crème fraîche and simmer, stirring continuously, for 3–4 minutes. Remove from the heat and instead of the herbs and butter, stir in 4–5 shredded sage leaves and 1 tablespoon lemon juice.

OPPOSITE, CLOCKWISE FROM TOP LEFT: VONGOLE WITH PASTA SHELLS, THREE-TOMATO SAUCE WITH PAPPARDELLE, CREAMY MUSHROOM SAUCE WITH RICCIOLI PASTA

SALSAS & OTHER FRESH SAUCES

AN INTERNATIONAL COLLECTION OF FRESH AND VERSATILE SALSAS AND SAUCES THAT ARE EASY TO PREPARE AND

REQUIRE VERY LITTLE COOKING, THESE CHUTNEYS, RELISHES, RAITAS, AND SAMBALS CAN ENLIVEN THE SIMPLEST

OF MEALS — SPOON THEM OVER BROILED FISH, MEAT, OR CHEESE, OR MIX THEM INTO PASTA, FOR EXAMPLE.

SERVE DIPS WITH PITA BREAD OR RAW VEGETABLES OR AS A LIGHT SNACK WITH A GLASS OF WINE.

SALSAS

THE WORD "SALSA" describes a large family of fresh or cooked salad-like relishes, usually flavored with chili and herbs. In Mexico, where the salsa evolved, they vary greatly in heat and spiciness, from the mild to the dangerously hot. Salsas can be served immediately but are much improved if left to marinate for a few hours.

THREE-CHILI SALSA

If you love chilies, this salsa is a must. Probably the hottest recipe in the book, this tart and fragrant salsa can be served spooned on top of broiled fish or chicken or simply as a dip with tortilla chips or crudités.

Shelf life: *1 week in the refrigerator*

¼lb (100g) mild red chilies, such as Anaheim, cubanelle, or fresno, roasted, peeled, seeded (see page 96), and sliced
....
2–3 red or green jalapeño chilies, seeded and thinly sliced
....
2–3 chipotle chilies, soaked in hot water for 25 minutes, drained, seeded, and chopped
....
1 large (250g) tomato, peeled, seeded (see page 43), and chopped
....
2 limes, peeled, sectioned, and chopped
....
grated peel and strained juice of 1 lime
....
4 tbsp chopped cilantro
....
salt

Mix all the ingredients together and let them marinate in the refrigerator for 1 hour before serving.

TOMATO & CUCUMBER SALSA ▷

1 large (250g) tomato, cubed
....
2 cups (250g) small, firm cucumbers, unpeeled, cubed
....
1 large red or white onion, finely chopped
....
1–2 green chilies, seeded, and finely chopped
....
1 tbsp chopped fresh marjoram, or 2 tsp dried
....
3–4 tbsp chopped fresh flat-leaf parsley or mint
....
3–4 tbsp olive oil
....
strained juice of 1 lemon, or to taste
....
salt

This brightly colored salsa is based on a traditional Arab salad. I serve this on a mound of hot bulgur or rice pilaf. It is also delicious with fish or chicken or as a tasty side salad.

Mix all the ingredients together in a bowl and let them marinate in the refrigerator for at least 1 hour.

OPPOSITE: FRESH TOMATO & CUCUMBER SALSA BEING TOSSED IN A BOWL

TOMATO & PEPPER SALSA

Serve this with any broiled meat or vegetables, as a piquant salad, or with pasta. You can make it in a food processor, but be careful not to overprocess – the vegetables should be finely chopped, not puréed. For a coarser texture, chop the ingredients by hand. The peppers can be replaced with avocado, banana, cucumber, or even chopped mango.

Shelf life: *1 week in the refrigerator; 6 months in a sealed jar (see pages 134–135)*

1½lb (750g) mixed green, red, and yellow peppers, seeded and coarsely chopped
2–3 fresh red or green chilies, seeded, and coarsely chopped
1 large red onion, coarsely chopped
2 garlic cloves, peeled
3 tbsp olive oil, corn oil, or peanut oil
3 tbsp red wine vinegar or lemon juice
2 tsp salt
1lb (500g) firm, ripe tomatoes, peeled, seeded (see page 43), and finely chopped
3 tbsp chopped cilantro or flat-leaf parsley (optional)

1 Put all the ingredients except the tomatoes and cilantro or parsley in a food processor and process, starting and stopping the machine, until the mixture is finely chopped but not puréed.

2 Transfer the mixture to a bowl and mix in the tomatoes and the cilantro or parsley, if using. If you are preserving the salsa, transfer the mixture to a pan and simmer for 5 minutes before packing into sterilized jars (see pages 134–35).

3 Otherwise, let it marinate in the refrigerator for 1 hour before serving.

PEELING PEPPERS & CHILIES

Either broil the peppers or chilies under a hot broiler or roast over an open flame until charred. Put them in a plastic bag for 5 minutes; then remove from the bag, hold under cold running water, and peel off the skin.

PAPAYA & KAFFIR LIME SALSA

1 green papaya, peeled, seeded, and coarsely grated
1–2 red Thai chilies, finely chopped
3 tbsp coconut cream
⅔ cup (150ml) coconut milk
4–5 kaffir lime leaves, finely chopped
strained juice of 1 large lime
grated peel of ½ lime
1–2 tsp palm sugar, jaggery (crushed), or light brown sugar
1–2 tbsp Thai fish sauce (*nam pla*)
2 tbsp coarsely chopped fresh cilantro

Green papaya adds a fresh and delicate flavor and crunchy texture to this salsa, which is particularly good served with smoked fish. Green papayas are available from Indian and Chinese groceries, but, if you can't find them unripe, green mango or a tart apple can be substituted. Coconut cream is available from Asian markets; it can also be skimmed off the top of coconut milk that has been left to stand.

Shelf life: *3–4 days in the refrigerator*

Mix all the ingredients together in a bowl, cover, and refrigerate for at least 2 hours before serving.

VARIATION

EXOTIC PAPAYA & KAFFIR LIME SALSA
Add 6 anchovy fillets, drained and cut into strips, or 3½oz (100g) rinsed and chopped salted herrings to the finished salsa. Serve as an accompaniment to chicken or fish.

BEET & APPLE SALSA

¼ cup (250g) raw or cooked beets, coarsely grated
2 cups (200g) apple, cored and cubed
1 onion, finely chopped
¾ cup (100g) cucumbers, chopped
4 tbsp red wine vinegar
2 tbsp mild olive, peanut, or sesame oil
1 tsp sugar
3 tbsp chopped fresh dill or flat-leaf parsley
salt and freshly ground black pepper

A fresh and delicious salsa that is good with cold cuts, pickled herring, or cheese. If you don't like raw beets, either cook them in water for about 45 minutes or, which I much prefer, roast them in an oven until tender.

Shelf life: *3–4 days in the refrigerator*

See page 21 for illustration

Mix all the ingredients together in a bowl and let them marinate in the refrigerator for at least 1 hour before serving.

TOMATILLO SALSA

Tomatillos, sometimes called Mexican green tomatoes, are available either fresh or canned in Mexican markets. Some cooks remove the small seeds, but I think they add an interesting and unique texture to the salsa.

Shelf life: *3–4 days in the refrigerator*

3½ cups (500g) tomatillos, husks removed, cubed

2–4 jalapeño chilies, roasted, peeled, seeded (see page 96), and finely chopped

1 white or yellow onion, finely chopped

strained juice of 2 limes and grated peel to taste

3 tbsp light olive oil or peanut oil

1–2 tbsp chopped cilantro or flat-leaf parsley

salt

Mix all the ingredients and let them marinate in the refrigerator for 1 hour.

POMEGRANATE & HERB SALSA

This is the simplest of salsas, wonderfully sharp and fresh in flavor. It is found in both Mexican and Persian cuisines and is superb with simple broiled fish.

Shelf life: *1 week in the refrigerator*

See pages 15 and 99 for illustration

1½ bunches each of fresh mint, flat-leaf parsley (leaves only), and cilantro, coarsely chopped

seeds of 1 pomegranate (see below)

1 small white onion, finely chopped

6 tbsp lime juice

grated peel of ½ lime

1–2 jalapeño or serrano chilies, finely chopped

2 tbsp peanut oil or olive oil

salt

Mix all the ingredients together in a bowl. Cover and chill for about 1 hour.

GUACAMOLE

3 ripe avocados, halved, pitted

1 white or red onion, finely chopped

1 large tomato, or 2 plum tomatoes, peeled, seeded (see page 43), and finely chopped

strained juice of 2 lemons or 4 limes, or to taste

grated lemon or lime peel to taste

1–3 fresh red chilies, seeded and finely chopped

1–2 tbsp chopped cilantro (optional)

salt

Scoop the avocado flesh into a bowl and mash coarsely with a fork, then mix in the rest of the ingredients. Squeeze a little more lemon or lime juice over the guacamole to prevent it from turning brown, then cover and refrigerate for about 30 minutes before serving.

The classic Mexican salsa. Use only completely ripe avocados, making sure you scrape out as much of the flesh as possible. I prefer my guacamole coarse in texture, but for smoother results use a food processor.

Shelf life: *3–4 days in the refrigerator*

REMOVING THE SEEDS FROM A POMEGRANATE

1 *Using a sharp knife, cut the ends off the pomegranate.*

2 *Make 4 equidistant cuts from the top to the bottom of the fruit.*

3 *Twist the pomegranate to break it into halves, then into quarters.*

4 *Press out the seeds, discarding any of the bitter membrane.*

MIXED PEPPER SALSA

Colorful, refreshing, and incredibly flavorful, this salsa is easily made in a food processor, but looks attractive if the ingredients are chopped by hand. Try chopping the peppers into julienne or matchsticks for really spectacular results.

Shelf life: *3–4 days in the refrigerator*

1 large red pepper, roasted, peeled, and seeded (see page 96)

1 large yellow or orange pepper, roasted, peeled, and seeded (see page 96)

1 large green pepper, roasted, peeled, and seeded (see page 96)

1 white or purple onion, finely chopped

1–3 jalapeño or Anaheim chilies, roasted, peeled, and seeded (see page 96)

6 tbsp lime juice or white wine vinegar

3–4 tbsp olive oil

3 tbsp shredded cilantro

salt

1 Put the peppers, onion, and chili in a food processor and process, starting and stopping the machine, until the mixture is finely chopped but not puréed.

2 Transfer the mixture to a bowl and add the rest of the ingredients. Mix well, cover, and chill before serving.

CITRUS SALSA

A tart and refreshing salsa with a hint of chili. I like to serve this with broiled or fried fish.

Shelf life: *3–4 days in the refrigerator*

2 oranges, peeled and sectioned, cut into ½ inch (1cm) pieces

2 large lemons, peeled and sectioned, cut into ½ inch (1cm) pieces

2 pickled lemons, seeded and finely chopped

1½ tsp chili flakes, or more to taste

2 tbsp paprika

3 tbsp chopped fresh flat-leaf parsley or mint

salt

Mix all the ingredients together in a bowl and let them marinate in the refrigerator for at least 1 hour before serving.

MANGO & TOMATO SALSA

1 ripe, firm mango, peeled, pitted, and cubed

1½ cups (300g) plum tomatoes, peeled (see page 43) and finely chopped

1 small white onion, finely chopped

2 garlic cloves, crushed

1–2 red chilies, finely chopped

5 tbsp lemon juice

grated peel of ½ lemon

2–3 tbsp torn fresh mint leaves or a mixture of mint and basil

1–2 tsp honey or sugar

salt

A fragrant, sweet and sour salsa that is fantastic with chicken. This is just as delicious if you substitute papaya for the mango.

Shelf life: *1 week in the refrigerator*

Mix all the ingredients in a bowl. Cover and chill well before serving.

ROAST CORN SALSA

2 ears of corn

1¾ cups (400g) plum tomatoes, roasted, peeled, seeded (see page 43), and finely chopped

2 jalapeño chilies, roasted, peeled, seeded (see page 96), and finely chopped

1 red onion, finely chopped

1 garlic clove, crushed

2–3 tbsp olive oil

juice of 1 lemon

grated peel of ½ lemon

1–2 tbsp torn cilantro

salt

A wonderfully smoky-flavored salsa that makes the perfect accompaniment to hamburgers. You could use frozen corn instead of fresh: simply roast it on a baking sheet in a hot oven until it starts to color.

Shelf life: *3–4 days in the refrigerator*

1 Broil or barbecue the corn for 20–30 minutes, or until golden. Cut the top off each ear of corn and stand it cut-side down on a chopping board. With a sharp knife, cut away the kernels, using the hard cob as a guide.

2 Put the kernels in a bowl and add the rest of the ingredients. Mix well; then cover and refrigerate for at least 2 hours before serving.

OPPOSITE, CLOCKWISE FROM TOP LEFT: MIXED PEPPER SALSA, MANGO & TOMATO SALSA, ROAST CORN SALSA, AND POMEGRANATE & HERB SALSA (SEE PAGE 97)

FRESH CHUTNEYS

IN INDIA, THE WORD "CHUTNEY" refers to a wide range of condiments from slow-cooked, jam-like preserves to more simple relishes made from freshly chopped raw vegetables that are ready to eat after marinating for a few hours. Chutneys can add flavor to snacks, cool down hot curries, or make an unusual sauce for rice or pasta.

FRESH ONION CHUTNEY

Select mild, sweet, and juicy onions for this fresh and simple chutney. Serve it as a side salad, to accompany pappadums or potato chips, or even as an interesting sandwich filling.

Shelf life: 1 day in the refrigerator

1lb (500g) large red or white sweet onions, sliced into thin rings
1 tbsp salt
1–2 green or red chilies, seeded and finely chopped
3 tbsp white wine vinegar or cider vinegar
2 tbsp chopped fresh mint or cilantro
1 tsp nigella seeds, dry-roasted (see page 78) (optional)

1 Put the onion rings in a colander and sprinkle with the salt. Mix well and let them drain for about 1 hour. Rinse; then squeeze any remaining moisture from the onions and pat dry.

2 Mix the rest of the ingredients together; add the onions and let the mixture stand for about 1 hour before serving.

COCONUT CHUTNEY

1 tbsp poppy seeds, dry-roasted (see page 78)
1 coconut, meat removed and finely grated, or 2¾ cups (250g) unsweetened flaked coconut, soaked in water for 20 minutes, then drained and squeezed dry
1 inch (2.5cm) fresh ginger, finely grated
1 small bunch of cilantro, finely chopped
1 tbsp jaggery, crushed, or sugar (optional)
1–2 green chilies, seeded and finely chopped
1 cup (200ml) coconut milk
strained lime or lemon juice to taste
salt

In southern India this chutney is made fresh daily. For a whiter, less fibrous chutney, remove the brown skin from the coconut flesh with a sharp knife or a potato peeler. If fresh coconut is not available, use unsweetened, flaked coconut or frozen shredded coconut, which is available in some Indian shops. Coconut chutney is the traditional accompaniment to samosas.

Shelf life: 1 week in the refrigerator

Mix all the ingredients together in a bowl and marinate for 1 hour before serving.

HERB CHUTNEY

The essence of spring and summer, this refreshing chutney is full of vitality. Try other fresh herbs such as flat-leaf parsley and dill. If using mint, use only the leaves and discard the tough stems.

1 large bunch of fresh mint or cilantro, chopped
1 bunch of scallions, finely chopped
1 tbsp sugar
1–2 green or red chilies, seeded and finely chopped
1 garlic clove, crushed
strained juice of 1–2 limes, or to taste
½ tsp chili powder, or to taste
salt

Mix all the ingredients together in a bowl and let them marinate in the refrigerator for no longer than 1 hour before serving. This is best eaten fresh.

CASHEW NUT CHUTNEY

1¼ cups (200g) cashew nuts
1 small onion, chopped
3 tbsp cilantro
1 inch (2.5cm) fresh ginger, chopped
2–3 green chilies, seeded and finely chopped
¼ tsp chili powder
1–2 tbsp lemon or lime juice (to taste)
salt

Traditionally, the ingredients for this chutney were pulverized in a stone mortar and pestle or with a grinding stone. Using a food processor is the modern equivalent, but the flavor is less intense and the texture different. For a nuttier flavor, roast the cashew nuts until golden.

Shelf life: 1 week in the refrigerator

Put the cashew nuts, onion, cilantro, and ginger into a food processor and process until smooth. Transfer to a bowl and stir in the remaining ingredients. Allow to marinate in the refrigerator for 1 hour.

GREEN CHILI CHUTNEY

Try this delicious, fresh-tasting, medium-hot chutney with vegetarian food or broiled or fried fish.

Shelf life: 3 weeks in the refrigerator; 1 month in a sealed jar (see pages 134–35)

10 (300g) long, thin, green chilies, stems removed, sliced in half lengthwise
3 tbsp salt
8 garlic cloves, peeled
1 inch (2.5cm) fresh ginger
3 tbsp mustard seeds
1 tbsp cumin seeds
¼ tsp asafoetida (optional)
½ cup (100ml) mustard oil, sesame oil, or peanut oil
1 tsp turmeric
1 tsp nigella seeds, dry-roasted (see page 78)
⅓ cup (100g) tamarind pulp soaked in 1 cup (200ml) hot vinegar, strained (see page 124)
3 tbsp jaggery, crushed, or brown sugar
salt

1 Place the chilies in a colander and sprinkle with the salt. Let them cure for about 3–4 hours. Wash off the excess salt, drain, and pat dry with paper towels.

2 Place the garlic, ginger, mustard seeds, cumin, and asafoetida, if using, in a spice mill or food processor and process to a smooth paste.

3 Heat the oil in a pan, add the turmeric and nigella, and fry for 2–3 minutes or until the mixture starts to emit a delicious aroma. Add the paste and fry for 5–8 minutes, until the mixture starts to brown. Add the tamarind vinegar, jaggery or brown sugar, and salt and simmer for a further 5–8 minutes, stirring and scraping the bottom of the pan until most of the liquid has evaporated.

4 Add the chilies, stir well, and simmer for 3–4 minutes. The chutney can be packed into sterilized jars at this point (see pages 134–35).

CARROT CHUTNEY

2½ cups (400g) carrots, coarsely grated
2 tsp salt
⅓ cup (75g) pistachio nuts, roasted in a dry pan until golden, finely chopped
1 bunch of scallions, finely chopped
2 inches (5cm) fresh ginger, grated
1 tbsp honey or brown sugar (optional)
⅓ cup (100g) tamarind pulp soaked in ½ cup (100ml) hot water, strained (see page 124)
1–2 red chilies, finely chopped
2 tsp nigella seeds, dry-roasted (see page 78)
3 tbsp chopped fresh dill or mint

1 Place the carrots in a colander, sprinkle with the salt, and let them drain for 1 hour. Rinse in cold water and drain well.

2 In a bowl, mix the carrots with all the remaining ingredients except the dill or mint. Add more salt, if necessary; then let the mixture marinate in the refrigerator for at least 1 hour. Sprinkle with the dill or mint just before serving.

Crunchy and refreshing, this chutney is especially good with hot curries such as vindaloo or madras. If a sweeter chutney is preferred, increase the amount of honey or sugar.

Shelf life: 1 week in the refrigerator

BANANA CHUTNEY

strained juice of 3 limes
¼ tsp chili powder
1 garlic clove, crushed
¼ tsp ground cardamom
¼ tsp asafoetida
3 ripe bananas, peeled and chopped
1 inch (2.5cm) fresh ginger, grated
1 bunch of scallions, finely chopped
2 limes, peeled and segments removed, chopped
1–2 chilies, seeded and finely chopped
salt

Mix the lime juice, chili powder, garlic, cardamom, and asafoetida together in a bowl. Stir in the rest of the ingredients; then cover and marinate for at least 1 hour before serving.

Novel and surprisingly delicious, this classic southern Indian chutney goes particularly well with fried or tandoori chicken (see page 110). You can also make it with ripe plantains.

Shelf life: 1 week in the refrigerator

RELISHES

RELISHES MAKE EASY WORK of cooking. Sweet, sour, fiery, or mellow, bright tasting relish will add interest to any dish. Serve them with hamburgers or barbecued meat, to enliven sandwiches and cold meat, or just as a versatile flavoring for sauces, mayonnaises, and soups. I have given large quantities for these relishes because they can easily be preserved for future use. I often make big batches of relish on rainy days.

MATBUCHA

A wonderfully tasty relish of Middle Eastern origin. Many other vegetables can be included – try adding chopped zucchini, pumpkin, butternut squash, or eggplant along with the peppers. If using canned tomatoes, always taste and adjust the sweet-sour balance by adding sugar, lemon juice, or vinegar to your liking.

Makes 3lb (1.5kg)

Shelf life: 3 weeks in the refrigerator; 6 months in a sealed jar (see pages 134–35)

1 cup (250ml) olive oil
1 tbsp cumin seeds or fennel seeds
2 large onions, chopped
1 large head of garlic, peeled and coarsely chopped
1 heart of a celery bunch with its leaves, finely chopped
4 red or green peppers, seeded and cut into thin ribbons
¾–1⅔ cups (75–150g) fresh red chilies, such as red jalapeño, seeded and chopped
3lb (1.5kg) cooking tomatoes, peeled, seeded, (see page 43), and coarsely chopped, or 3 x 18oz cans (3kg) tomatoes, drained
3 tbsp tomato paste
lemon juice to taste (optional)
1 tbsp sugar (optional)
salt

1 Heat the oil in a large pan. Add the cumin or fennel seeds and toast for 2–3 minutes, or until they give off a pleasant nutty aroma. Add the onions, garlic, and celery and cook gently for about 8 minutes, or until the onions are translucent, then add the peppers and chilies and fry for a further 5 minutes.

2 Add the tomatoes and tomato paste. Reduce the heat and, with the pan partially covered, simmer, stirring occasionally, for about 1½ hours, or until most of the liquid has evaporated and the relish has thickened. Taste; then stir in some lemon juice and the sugar, if necessary, and season with salt. The relish can be transferred to sterilized jars (see pages 134–35), if desired.

GREEN CHILI RELISH

3 tbsp olive oil
1 cup (250g) white or yellow onions, finely chopped
6 garlic cloves, chopped
1lb (500g) jalapeño or serrano chilies, roasted, peeled, and seeded (see page 96), finely chopped
1 tbsp dried oregano
1 cup (250ml) white wine vinegar, cider vinegar, or distilled vinegar
1 cup (250ml) water
1 scant tbsp salt
1 tbsp flour mixed with 2 tbsp light oil

This is a superb, fiery-hot South American chili relish. It is used to flavor soups, salsas, or mayonnaise, or to top hamburgers, broiled chicken, or other meat.

Makes 1½lb (750g)

Shelf life: 3 weeks in the refrigerator; 6 months in a sealed jar (see pages 134–35)

1 Heat the oil in a pan, add the onions and garlic and sauté gently for about 5 minutes, or until the onions are translucent. Add the chilies, oregano, vinegar, water, and salt and bring to a boil. Reduce the heat and simmer for about 20 minutes. If a smooth relish is preferred, process in a food processor, then return the mixture to the pan.

2 Add the flour and oil mixture and mix well. Bring to a boil and cook for 5–8 minutes, stirring frequently, until the relish has thickened. The relish can be preserved (see pages 134–35), if desired.

HARISSA

Here is the recipe for this famous, fiercely hot Moroccan chili sauce. You may like to tame its hotness by adding a little Tomato Paste (see page 43). About a tablespoon of dry-roasted cumin seeds can be added too.

Makes 1lb (500g)

Shelf life: 3 months in the refrigerator; 1 year in a sealed jar (make sure the surface of the paste is covered by a thin layer of oil)

See page 15 for illustration

8 cups (500g) dried red chilies, stems removed

⅓ cup (100g) garlic

1 tbsp coriander seeds, dry-roasted (see page 78) and ground

⅔ cup (150ml) olive oil

1½ tbsp salt

1 Put the chilies in a bowl; add enough hot water to cover them and let them stand for 15–20 minutes until soft.

2 Drain the chilies and place in a food processor with about ½ cup (125ml) of the soaking water. Process to form a paste, add the garlic, coriander seeds, oil, and salt, and process. The harissa can be used immediately or can be packed into sterilized jars (see pages 134–35).

FRUITY CHILI RELISH

A deliciously hot relish, perfect with cold chicken, meat, or mature cheeses; it can also be spread thickly over broiled lamb chops and caramelized under a hot broiler.

Makes 1lb 13oz (900g)

Shelf life: 3 months in the refrigerator; 1 year in sealed jars

1lb (500g) mangoes, peeled, pitted, and coarsely chopped

2 large sweet apples, peeled, cored, and coarsely chopped

2 onions, chopped

2⅓ cups (200g) red chilies, seeded and chopped

1 cup (200g) sugar

1 cup (250ml) cider vinegar or wine vinegar

1 large bunch cilantro, chopped

salt

1 Place the mangoes, apples, onions, and chilies in a food processor and process until finely chopped but not puréed.

2 Transfer the chopped ingredients to a large pan and add the sugar. Cook over high heat for 8–10 minutes, or until most of the liquid has evaporated and the sugar is a pale caramel color.

3 Mix in the vinegar and cilantro and boil for 4–5 minutes, until the mixture is jam-like. Season with salt; preserve in sterilized jars (see pages 134–35), if desired.

TWO-TOMATO RELISH

2lb (1kg) cherry tomatoes

3½ cups (200g) sun-dried tomatoes in oil, chopped, oil reserved, and extra olive oil added, if necessary, to make ⅔ cup (150ml)

1¼ cups (150g) onions, chopped

6 garlic cloves, coarsely chopped

3 tbsp chopped fresh thyme

1–2 red chilies, seeded and finely chopped

strained juice of 2 lemons

1–2 tbsp dark brown sugar (optional)

salt

Put all the ingredients in a deep roasting pan and roast in an oven preheated to 450°F/230°C for about 45 minutes–1 hour, or until most of the liquid has evaporated. Store in sterilized jars (see pages 134–35), if desired.

Sun-dried tomatoes give a sunny Mediterranean flavor to this tasty, piquant relish.

Makes 1lb 3½oz (600g)

Shelf life: 3 weeks refrigerated; 6 months in sealed jars

See page 17 for illustration

EXOTIC FRUIT RELISH

1 cup (250g) palm or unrefined sugar

⅓ cup (90ml) rice or white wine vinegar

1 small pineapple, peeled and finely chopped

2 inches (5cm) fresh ginger, finely shredded

3–4 red chilies, seeded and finely chopped

6 garlic cloves, chopped

5 kaffir lime leaves

1 small bunch cilantro, chopped

2–3 tbsp Thai fish sauce (*nam pla*)

1 Put the sugar and vinegar in a pan and boil until the sugar dissolves and begins to caramelize.

2 Carefully add (hot steam will be created) all the remaining ingredients except the fish sauce to the caramelized mixture and mix well.

3 Bring to a boil; add the fish sauce and cook for 5 minutes, or until the relish is thick and jam-like. Preserve in sterilized jars (see pages 134–35), if desired.

This is a superbly fragrant relish inspired by the flavors of Southeast Asian cooking. Serve this with chicken, fish, or seafood. Mango or papaya can be substituted for the pineapple.

Makes 1lb (500g)

Shelf life: 3 months in the refrigerator; 1 year in sealed jars

See page 13 for illustration

RAITAS & SAMBALS

A LARGE FAMILY OF YOGURT-BASED SALADS, raitas are served as cooling accompaniments to hot curries or to add moisture to dry dishes. For a light, fresh summer main course, pour chilled raita over pasta or bulgur pilaf.

Sambals are a range of fresh salads and relishes that originated in Southeast Asia but were developed by the Cape Malays in South Africa. Serve them with broiled meat, curries, or rice pilafs.

ONION RAITA

This is a fresh, crunchy raita to be served with hot curries.

Shelf life: *1 day in the refrigerator*

4 onions, halved and thinly sliced
1 tbsp sugar or jaggery, crushed
1 cup (250ml) yogurt
strained juice of 1/2 lemon
1 tsp nigella seeds, dry-roasted (see page 78)
1/4 tsp chili powder or finely chopped fresh chili (optional)
4 tbsp chopped fresh mint or cilantro
salt and freshly ground black pepper

1 Place the onions in a colander, sprinkle the sugar or jaggery over them, and set aside to drain for about 1 hour. Squeeze out any excess liquid.

2 Mix the onions with the rest of the ingredients in a bowl and chill for at least 1 hour before serving.

TOMATO RAITA

Serve this with hot curries or as a cool dip with papadums. For a cucumber raita, substitute the same amount of chopped cucumber and use dry-roasted fennel seeds instead of cumin seeds.

Shelf life: *1 day in the refrigerator*

See page 17 for illustration

1 1/2 cups (350g) plum tomatoes, peeled, seeded (see page 45), and chopped
1 bunch of scallions, chopped
1 cup (250ml) yogurt
strained juice of 2 limes or 1 large lemon
a few gratings of lime or lemon peel
1/4 tsp chili powder or 1 small chili, chopped
1 tsp cumin seeds, dry-roasted (see page 78)
4 tbsp chopped fresh mint or cilantro
salt

Mix all the ingredients together in a bowl. Chill for at least 1 hour before serving.

QUINCE SAMBAL

I like to serve this deliciously fragrant, autumnal sambal with broiled fish or curry.

Shelf life: *3 days in the refrigerator*

2 cups (400g) ripe quinces, peeled and coarsely grated
2 tsp salt
2 inches (5cm) fresh ginger, finely grated
1–2 green chilies, seeded and chopped
strained juice of 2 lemons
a few gratings of lemon peel

1 Put the quinces in a colander and sprinkle salt over them. Let them drain for about 1 hour. Squeeze out any excess liquid with your hands.

2 In a bowl mix the quinces with the remaining ingredients. Taste the mixture and add a little more salt if necessary, then set aside to marinate for 1 hour before serving.

VARIATION

CARROT SAMBAL
Substitute 2 cups grated carrots for the quinces and 1 bunch of chopped scallions for the ginger. Omit the lemon juice and peel and add 3 tablespoons white wine vinegar or cider vinegar.

CUCUMBER SAMBAL

Originally, this sambal was flavored with fermented fish or shrimp paste (blatjang), but I find that salted anchovies make a very good substitute.

Shelf life: *3 days in the refrigerator*

2 1/2 cups (500g) firm cucumbers, coarsely grated
1 small onion, finely grated
6 anchovy fillets in oil, drained, finely chopped
2 green or red chilies, seeded and finely chopped
3 tbsp white wine vinegar

Combine all the ingredients in a bowl and chill for about 1 hour or so before serving.

DIPS

THESE RECIPES ARE PREDOMINANTLY Mediterranean in origin. They can be served as part of a mezze – a collection of small, fresh or cooked, dishes designed to whet the appetite – or eaten as a light snack with a glass of wine or an apéritif. Make sure the dips are well chilled. Accompany them with a selection of fresh leaves, such as chicory or lettuce, sticks of raw vegetables, and toast, chips, or warm pita bread.

SMOKY EGGPLANT DIP

The bland flavor of eggplant makes it an ideal base for dips. You can cook the eggplant in a very hot oven or under a hot broiler, but for a good smoky flavor, roast directly on an open gas flame or on a barbecue grill. For a smooth dip, purée the eggplant in a food processor. I sometimes stir in 6 tablespoons of tahini – which adds a slightly nutty flavor – and a little extra lemon juice.

Shelf life: 1 week in the refrigerator

2–3 large eggplants
1 large white or red onion, or 1 bunch scallions, chopped
2–3 garlic cloves, crushed
4–6 tbsp virgin olive oil
strained juice of 1–2 lemons, to taste
a few gratings of lemon peel
1–2 red or green chilies, seeded and finely chopped
4–5 tbsp chopped fresh parsley, mint, or sweet marjoram, or a combination of all 3
salt

1 Roast or broil the eggplants until the skin is charred and the flesh is soft, about 10–15 minutes. Make a deep gash in each; then place in a colander until cool enough to handle. Peel the eggplants under cold running water, removing as much of the charred skin as possible.

2 Chop the eggplant flesh coarsely and return to the colander. Sprinkle with 1 teaspoon salt; then cover and allow to drain for at least 1 hour. (You can speed up this process by gently squeezing the water from the eggplant flesh.)

3 Place the flesh on a chopping board and chop with a large knife or a mezzaluna (double-handed herb chopper) until puréed but still textured. Transfer to a bowl and mix in the remaining ingredients. Chill well before serving.

VARIATIONS

PEPPER & EGGPLANT DIP
Add 3 roasted and peeled (see page 96) red or mixed color peppers to the finished eggplant dip.

FETA & EGGPLANT DIP
Stir in 1½ cups (200g) crumbled feta cheese and ½ cup (100g) peeled, seeded (see page 43), and chopped tomatoes.

YOGURT, GARLIC, & LEMON DIP

A fragrant, low-calorie dip that is especially good with seafood or vegetables.

Shelf life: 1 day in the refrigerator

1¼ cups (300ml) regular or low-fat yogurt
1 pickled lemon, finely chopped
1 garlic clove, crushed
2 tbsp olive oil
1–2 red chilies, finely chopped
2 tsp sweet paprika
3 tbsp chopped fresh dill or mint
salt

Mix all the ingredients together in a bowl and chill well before serving.

VARIATION

SIMPLE YOGURT DIP
For a simple and versatile yogurt dip, substitute the juice of 1 lemon and a few gratings of lemon peel for the pickled lemon and fresh mint, parsley, or cilantro for the dill. Omit the chilies and paprika and add 3 tablespoons of either capers, pitted olives, anchovies, sun-dried tomatoes, or cucumbers. Season with salt and pepper.

BEAN DIP

This is a delicious, slightly nutty-flavored dip to serve with raw vegetables, potato chips, tortilla chips, or warmed pita bread.

Shelf life: 3 days in the refrigerator

1 cup (200g) dried navy beans
4 tbsp extra-virgin olive oil
1 large onion, finely chopped
strained juice of 1 large lemon
3 tbsp chopped fresh flat-leaf parsley or mint
salt and freshly ground black pepper

1 Soak the beans overnight in enough cold water to cover them. Drain; then boil them in plenty of water until soft, about 1 hour. Drain well, reserving the cooking liquid.

2 Place the beans in a food processor and process to a smooth purée with a little of the cooking liquid.

3 Heat the oil in a frying pan, add the onion, and fry until crisp and golden brown, about 10–15 minutes.

4 Transfer the bean purée to a bowl, add the fried onion, and mix in the rest of the ingredients. Add a little more cooking liquid if the mixture is too thick. Serve warm or at room temperature.

PEPPER DIP

For smoother results, make this dip in a food processor. I sometimes roast and peel the peppers (see page 96), which gives the dip a more pronounced flavor.

Shelf life: 3 days in the refrigerator

1 cup (250g) fromage frais, or cottage cheese diluted with a little milk or yogurt
3 peppers, preferably red, yellow, and green, cored, seeded, and finely chopped
1–2 red or green chilies, seeded and finely chopped (optional)
4–5 scallions, finely chopped
1 tsp caraway seeds, coarsely ground
3 tbsp chopped fresh dill
strained juice of 1 lemon, or to taste
salt and freshly ground black pepper

Mix all the ingredients together in a bowl or food processor and refrigerate for at least 2 hours before serving.

TARAMASALATA

5oz (150g) smoked cod roe, or 4oz (125g) tarama paste
1 small onion, finely grated
5 slices (150g) crustless white bread, soaked in water and squeezed dry
strained juice of 1 lemon, or more to taste
grated peel of ½ lemon (optional)
1 small garlic clove, crushed (optional)
1–1¼ cups (250–300ml) extra-virgin olive oil, or a mixture of olive and peanut oil

Smooth and delicately pink, this famous Greek dip can be diluted with a little lemon juice, water, or milk and served as a piquant sauce with broiled fish or seafood.

Shelf life: 3 days in the refrigerator

1 If using cod roe, put it in a bowl, pour boiling water over it, and soak for 5 minutes. Drain, refresh with cold water, then peel off and discard the membrane.

2 Put the cod roe or tarama paste, onion, bread, lemon juice and peel, and garlic, if using, in a food processor and process until smooth. With the machine running, add the oil in a thin, steady stream; process until the consistency of heavy cream.

SOUR CREAM & SAFFRON DIP

2 tbsp (30g) butter or olive oil
½ cup (100g) shallots, finely chopped
½ cup (125ml) dry white wine
¼ tsp saffron strands, soaked in 2 tbsp warm water or white wine
1 cup (250ml) sour cream or crème fraîche
1–2 tbsp lemon juice, or to taste
salt

With a delicate golden color, this dip goes particularly well with shrimp or raw vegetables. For a spicier dip, use 1–2 tablespoons of curry powder instead of the saffron.

Shelf life: 3 days in the refrigerator

1 Heat the butter or olive oil in a small pan; add the shallots and fry until golden. Add the wine and the saffron mixture and bring to a boil. Reduce the heat and simmer until most of the liquid has evaporated, about 10 minutes. Remove from the heat and allow to cool.

2 In a bowl, mix the cooled shallot mixture with the remaining ingredients. Chill for at least 1 hour before serving.

OPPOSITE, CLOCKWISE FROM TOP LEFT: BEAN DIP, TARAMASALATA, SOUR CREAM & SAFFRON DIP, AND PEPPER DIP

MARINADES & SPICE PASTES

THESE HERB- AND SPICE-PACKED MARINADES AND PASTES ARE A CONVENIENT WAY TO INTRODUCE

FLAVOR, TENDERIZE TOUGH CUTS OF MEAT, AND TURN SIMPLE FOODS INTO SPECIAL TREATS WITH A MINIMUM

OF FUSS. MARINATING TIME IS DETERMINED BY THE THICKNESS OF THE FOOD BEING MARINATED – THE

THICKER IT IS, THE MORE TIME IS NEEDED FOR THE FLAVORS TO PENETRATE. POUR THE MARINADE OVER THE

FOOD AND PLACE IT IN THE REFRIGERATOR. TURN THE FOOD IN THE MARINADE FROM TIME TO TIME

TO MAKE SURE IT IS EVENLY AND THOROUGHLY COATED.

FRESH HERB LAMB MARINADE

I have tried many versions of this aromatic marinade, changing the herbs according to their availability. Any fragrant herb can be used, but my favorite is lavender – both the leaves and the flowering heads. This is a delicious marinade for lamb kebabs.

Enough for 2lb (1kg) lamb

Marinating time:
5–24 hours

4–5 garlic cloves

1 small onion, roughly chopped

⅔ cup (150ml) olive oil

juice and grated peel of 1 large lemon (peel optional)

about 6 cups (100g) coarsely chopped or bruised fresh herbs of your choice, such as lavender leaves and flowering heads, wild or garden thyme, rosemary, or wild marjoram

salt and coarsely ground black pepper

1 Place the garlic and onion in a food processor and process to a smooth paste. Add the olive oil, lemon juice and peel, if using, and process. Add the herbs and salt and pepper.

2 Pour the marinade over the meat, cover, and marinate in the refrigerator.

MEDITERRANEAN FISH MARINADE ▷

juice of 1–2 lemons

grated peel of 1 lemon

6 tbsp good olive oil

2 garlic cloves, crushed

1 tsp black peppercorns, crushed

1 tsp fennel seeds, dry-roasted (see page 78) and crushed

1 small bunch of fresh parsley, dill, or wild fennel tops, finely chopped

salt

Mix all the ingredients together in a bowl. Make 3 slashes on each side of the fish, then pour the marinade over the fish in a shallow bowl. Cover and allow to marinate in the refrigerator before broiling, baking, or frying the fish.

This is especially delicious as a marinade for whole fish such as bass or tuna, or gray or red mullet. It is also good with fatty fish such as mackerel or sardines.

Enough for 2lb (1kg) fish

Marinating time:
2–4 hours

See page 11 for illustration

CIDER & HERB MARINADE

This is wonderful for pork chops or large pieces of pork, and also for chicken, duck, or rabbit. If the marinade doesn't cover the meat, turn it from time to time to make sure it is thoroughly coated.

Enough for 4–6lb (2–3kg) meat

Marinating time: 12 hours; 3 days for larger pieces of meat

4 cups (1 liter) cider
⅖ cup (100ml) cider vinegar
3 tbsp honey or sugar
2 tart apples, chopped or grated
2 celery stalks, chopped
1 small bunch of fresh thyme, bruised
6–8 fresh sage leaves, bruised
2 bay leaves
1 tbsp coriander seeds, crushed
½ tsp cloves, crushed
1 tsp black peppercorns, crushed

Mix all the ingredients together, pour them over the meat in a shallow dish, and allow to marinate in the refrigerator.

TRADITIONAL BARBECUE SAUCE

One of the cornerstones of North American barbecue culture, this versatile sauce is used to marinate beef, chicken, ribs, or pork. It is good for basting meats while cooking and can also be served as a side sauce for many broiled and barbecued dishes.

Enough for about 4lb (2kg) meat

Marinating time: 2–24 hours

Shelf life: 6 months in a sealed jar (see pages 134–135)

4 tbsp peanut or sesame oil
1 large onion, finely chopped
4 garlic cloves, finely chopped
1 tbsp chili powder
2 cups (500ml) tomato ketchup
1 cup (250ml) cider vinegar
4 tbsp lemon juice
4 tbsp Worcestershire sauce
5 tbsp soft dark brown sugar
1 tbsp celery seeds, crushed

1 Heat the oil in a pan; add the onion and garlic and sauté gently until the onion is golden and soft.

2 Add the rest of the ingredients, bring to a boil; then reduce the heat and simmer for 30 minutes. Set aside to cool a little; then pour over the meat. Allow to cool completely, cover, and marinate in the refrigerator. The sauce can be preserved, if desired (see pages 134–35).

TANDOORI MARINADE

6 garlic cloves
2 inches (5cm) fresh ginger
1 cup (250ml) yogurt
juice of 2 limes or 1 lemon
grated peel of ½ lime
2 tbsp ground coriander
1 tbsp sweet paprika
1 tbsp ground cumin
1 tbsp ground turmeric
1–2 tsp chili powder
½ tsp ground cardamom
1 tbsp salt

Traditionally, tandoori marinade is bright red, but this effect is achieved with artificial coloring. I prefer tandoori to be the natural color of the aromatic spices it contains.

Enough for about 2–3lb (1–1.5kg) skinless chicken pieces or lamb chops

Marinating time: 12–24 hours

See page 19 for illustration

1 Place the garlic and ginger in a spice mill or food processor and process to a smooth paste. Add the rest of the ingredients and process until well mixed.

2 Pour the marinade over chicken or lamb pieces in a shallow dish; cover and refrigerate. Bake in a clay tandoor, in a hot oven, or, alternatively, broil or barbecue.

BARBECUE SAUCE WITH COCOA

4 tbsp cocoa powder
1 cup (250ml) red wine vinegar
1 cup (200g) tomato paste
8 tbsp honey or ½ cup (100g) dark brown sugar
2 tbsp olive oil
10 garlic cloves, crushed
3–4 fresh red chilies, finely chopped, or chili powder to taste (optional)
1 tbsp dried oregano (optional)
2 tbsp soy sauce
salt to taste

Cocoa powder is an unusual addition to this classic sauce, but it gives an intensity of flavor and a wonderful dark color. Use it to marinate, as a baste for barbecuing, or simply as a dipping sauce for barbecued meat or vegetables.

Enough for 4lb (2kg) meat

Marinating time: 2–24 hours

Shelf life: 6 months in sealed jars

Dissolve the cocoa powder in a little of the vinegar; place in a pan with the rest of the ingredients. Bring to a boil; then reduce the heat and simmer, stirring, for 20 minutes. Use to marinate meat in the refrigerator, or preserve, if desired (see pages 134–35).

ORANGE & GINGER SAUCE ▷

A tangy, slightly sharp-tasting sauce that goes very well with pork, duck, and chicken. It can be used as a marinade or for basting meat while cooking, or even as a side sauce. This is really delicious with pork or chicken kebabs.

Enough for 4lb (2kg) meat

Marinating time:
4–24 hours for pork;
3–4 hours for chicken;
4–5 hours for duck

Shelf life: 6 months in sealed jars

2 cups (500ml) orange juice
grated peel of 1 orange
4 tbsp tomato paste
⅓ cup (75ml) tomato ketchup
⅓ cup (75ml) cider vinegar or white wine vinegar
4 tbsp olive oil
3 tbsp dark soy sauce
4 tbsp molasses
4 garlic cloves, crushed or processed to a smooth paste
1 small onion, finely grated or processed to a smooth paste
2 inches (5cm) ginger, finely grated or processed to a smooth paste
1–2 fresh, hot red chilies, seeded and finely chopped, or chili powder to taste
1 tsp cornstarch, dissolved in 2 tbsp vinegar (optional)
salt

Put the orange juice in a pan and bring to a boil, skimming any foam from the surface. Boil until reduced by half; then add all the rest of the ingredients except the cornstarch, if using, and simmer for 20 minutes. If the sauce is too thin, add the cornstarch and boil until it thickens. Use for marinating or basting, or preserve, if desired (see pages 134–35).

BEER MARINADE

Use this to marinate cuts of beef, wild boar, or venison.

Enough for a 2–4lb (1–2kg) cut of meat

Marinating time:
12 hours – 2 days

3¼ cups (750ml) good, flavorsome ale or beer
5 tbsp brown sugar
4 tbsp malt vinegar
1 tbsp allspice berries, crushed
1 small bunch of fresh thyme, chopped
2–3 bay leaves

Mix all the ingredients together in a large, shallow dish. Add the meat, cover, and allow to marinate in the refrigerator; then roast as normal.

RIGHT: ORANGE & GINGER SAUCE ON A PORK KEBAB

◁ CEVICHE

strained juice of 3 limes
grated peel of 1 lime
½ cup (100g) plum tomatoes, peeled, seeded (see page 43), and finely chopped
1 small red or sweet white onion, finely chopped
1–3 green or red chilies, seeded and finely chopped
3 tbsp light olive or peanut oil
1–2 fresh lime or lemon leaves, finely shredded (optional)
2 tsp salt
3 tbsp chopped cilantro or flat-leaf parsley

A delicious, light, and tangy marinade for raw fish salad. The fresh lime juice "cooks" the fish. Use very fresh fish steaks such as tuna, swordfish, barramundi, or salmon.

Enough for 1lb (500g) skinless fish steaks, cut into cubes

Marinating time: 2–24 hours

Shelf life: 24 hours in the refrigerator

Mix all the ingredients except the cilantro or parsley together; then pour over cubed fish in a bowl. Cover and allow to marinate in the refrigerator. Stir in the cilantro or parsley just before serving.

TZARAMELO

strained juice of 2 lemons
grated peel of ½ lemon
2 plum tomatoes, peeled, seeded (see page 43), and finely chopped
2 garlic cloves, finely chopped
1 green pepper, seeded and finely chopped
1–2 red or green chilies, finely chopped, or chili powder to taste (optional)
1 small red or white onion, finely chopped
1 small bunch of fresh dill, snipped
salt and freshly ground black pepper

This Mediterranean marinade is delicious with fried fish such as red mullet and is also good with chicken. It should be poured over hot fish or meat.

Enough for 3–4lb (1.5–2kg) fish or chicken

Marinating time: 5–10 minutes, turning the fish or meat frequently to make sure it is evenly coated

Mix all the ingredients together in a bowl. Pour the marinade over hot broiled or fried fish or chicken and allow to marinate before serving.

LEFT: SUCCULENT CUBES OF SWORDFISH IN A ZESTY CEVICHE

ORIENTAL SOY MARINADE

Adapt this recipe to your own taste by adding flavorings such as scallions, lemongrass, shallots, and different herbs and spices. Use the marinade for chicken pieces, beefsteak cubes, or cubed tofu.

Enough to marinate 1lb (500g) chicken pieces, steak, or tofu

Marinating time: 4 hours

6 tbsp dark soy sauce
2 tbsp soft dark brown sugar
3 star anise, crushed
2 garlic cloves, crushed
2 inches (5cm) fresh ginger, chopped (optional)
1–2 fresh chilies, chopped (optional)

Mix all the ingredients together and pour over meat or cubed tofu in a shallow dish. Cover and marinate in the refrigerator.

LEMON & CHILI MARINADE

This marinade should be poured over cooked fish, such as bass, snapper, or swordfish steaks. It is also delicious with chicken.

Enough for 2–3lb (1–1.5kg) fish or chicken

Marinating time: 5–10 minutes, turning the fish or chicken from time to time to make sure it is evenly coated

juice of 1 large lemon and grated peel of ½
3 tbsp water
3 garlic cloves, crushed
3 tbsp fruity olive oil
1 tbsp, or more to taste, Harissa (see page 103) or chopped fresh chili
2 tsp sweet paprika
½ large bunch of fresh parsley, chopped
salt

Mix all the ingredients together in a bowl; pour over hot fish or chicken to marinate.

APRICOT & HERB MARINADE

This is delicious on pork chops or steaks; it should be poured over the meat while it is still hot and allowed to marinate only briefly.

Enough for 2lb (1kg) pork chops or steaks

Marinating time: 5–10 minutes, turning the meat from time to time to make sure it is evenly coated

4 tbsp apricot jam
⅖ cup (100ml) white wine or dry cider
4–5 fresh sage leaves, chopped, or 1–2 tbsp chopped fresh rosemary
3 tbsp rum
salt and freshly ground black pepper

Place the jam and wine or cider in a pan and bring to a boil. Reduce the heat and simmer, stirring, for 1–2 minutes to melt the jam. Remove from the heat and add the remaining ingredients; then pour the marinade over broiled or fried pork chops or steaks and allow to marinate.

CHIMICHURRI

5 garlic cloves, crushed
1–2 or more red jalapeño or Anaheim chilies, seeded and finely chopped
5 tbsp red wine vinegar
½ cup (125ml) olive oil
4 tbsp finely chopped fresh oregano or 1 tbsp dried oregano
1 bunch of cilantro or flat-leaf parsley, finely chopped
salt

A hot and spicy Mexican marinade for pork or beef that can also be used as a basting sauce or a dip. You can use a food processor or a blender to purée the ingredients instead of chopping them by hand.

Enough for 4lb (2kg) meat

Marinating time: 2–12 hours

Combine all the ingredients in a bowl, add the meat, coating it in the mixture, and leave to marinate in the refrigerator.

SOUTH AFRICAN SOSATIE

¼ cup (50ml) peanut or light olive oil
1lb (500g) onions, thinly sliced
2 inches (5cm) fresh ginger, chopped
3 garlic cloves, chopped
1–2 tbsp curry powder
⅖ cup (100g) tamarind pulp, soaked in 1¼ cups (300ml) hot water or red wine vinegar, sieved (see page 124)
1–2 lemon, orange, or kaffir lime leaves, finely shredded
salt

Mildly curry-flavored, this marinade is traditionally used with lamb but is also good with beef or chicken. For a pleasant fruity edge, add 1–2 tablespoons of apricot chutney with the tamarind water.

Enough for 2lb (1kg) meat

Marinating time: 12 hours

See page 13 for illustration

1 Heat the oil in a large frying pan; add the onions and fry for 8–10 minutes, or until lightly browned. Add the rest of the ingredients and bring to a boil; then remove from the heat and set aside to cool.

2 Pour the cooled marinade over the meat and allow to marinate in the refrigerator for 12 hours; then lift out and barbecue the meat, using a little of the marinade for basting.

3 Place the remaining marinade in a pan, bring to a boil, and simmer gently until most of the liquid has evaporated. Serve the reduced onion mixture on top of the barbecued meat.

HERB PASTE FOR FISH

This gives a fresh, tangy flavor to baked sea bass, salmon, snapper, or any other large fish; it also keeps the fish wonderfully moist.

Enough for a 2–3lb (1–1.5kg) fish

Marinating time: 30 minutes – 1 hour

4 tbsp (60g) butter
2 tbsp olive oil
¼ tsp fennel seeds
⅔ cup (150g) shallots, or 1 onion, chopped
1 inch (2.5cm) fresh ginger, minced
2oz (60g) can of anchovies, drained and chopped
1 small bunch of fresh dill, finely chopped
1 small bunch of fresh parsley, finely chopped
1 tbsp capers, drained and rinsed
juice and grated peel of ½ lemon
3 tbsp breadcrumbs

1 Heat the butter and olive oil in a skillet, add the fennel seeds, and fry gently for a few minutes. Add the shallots or onion and the ginger and cook until they start to change color, about 5–8 minutes. Remove from the heat and stir in the rest of the ingredients.

2 Cut the fish open and use the paste as a stuffing. Pile the rest over the fish in an ovenproof baking dish. Marinate in the refrigerator; then bake as normal.

PASTE FOR COOKED MEATS

A superb way of adding flavor to cold cooked meat. I use it for broiled bacon, pork roasts, beef brisket, or cooked or cured turkey breast.

Enough for 2–3lb (1–1.5kg) meat

Marinating time: at least 2 days

Shelf life: 1 week in the refrigerator

28 garlic cloves, peeled
4 tbsp sweet Hungarian paprika
1–2 tsp hot Hungarian paprika or chili powder
1 tbsp salt
2 tbsp caraway seeds, finely ground
1 tbsp freshly ground black pepper
2 tbsp olive oil

1 Process the garlic to a paste in a food processor; then mix with all the remaining ingredients.

2 Spread a thick coating of the paste all over the cooked meat; then allow to marinate in an airtight container in the refrigerator. Cut into thin slices to serve.

PAPAYA MARINATING PASTE

1 small (100–150g) unripe papaya, peeled, halved, seeded, and coarsely chopped
the papaya seeds, crushed to a paste
½ cup (100ml) coconut milk or water
2 inches (5cm) fresh ginger, chopped
2 lemongrass stalks, hard outer layers removed, chopped
1–2 fresh chilies, or chili powder to taste
salt

Place all the ingredients in a food processor and process to a smooth paste. Cover the meat in the paste and marinate in the refrigerator.

Unripe green papayas contain a large amount of an enzyme that tenderizes meat. This puréed papaya paste works very well on tough cuts of meat such as beef or mutton. Fresh pineapple can be used instead of the papaya.

Enough for 2lbs (1kg) meat

Marinating time: up to 12 hours

JAMAICAN JERK PASTE

1 onion, peeled and quartered
6 garlic cloves
20 (250g) Habañero chilies, seeded
8 inches (100g) fresh ginger, peeled
1 small bunch of fresh flat-leaf parsley
1 bunch of scallions
4 tbsp ground allspice
1 cup (60g) fresh thyme, chopped, or 2 tbsp dried thyme
1 tsp ground cloves
2–3 tbsp dark soy sauce
strained juice of 3 limes

Purée the first 6 ingredients in a food processor, then add the remaining ingredients and process to mix. Pour the mixture over the meat in a shallow dish and marinate in the refrigerator.

This recipe is said to have been developed by runaway slaves in Jamaica. Habañero chilies are dangerously hot; I advise wearing gloves when handling them.

Enough for 2–3lb (1–1.5kg) meat

Marinating time: 12–24 hours

Shelf life: 1 week in the refrigerator; 3 months in the freezer; 6 months in sealed jars (see pages 134–35)

NORTH AFRICAN SPICE PASTE

A wonderfully fragrant paste that is very good with broiled or barbecued chicken, lamb, or pork chops. Fragrant and strongly flavored, preserved lemons are popular in North African cooking – look for them in North African and Middle Eastern grocers.

Enough for about 3–4lb (1.5–2kg) meat

Marinating time: 12–24 hours

8 garlic cloves, crushed
2 preserved lemons with seeds removed, finely chopped
1 inch (2.5cm) fresh ginger, chopped
2 tsp salt
½ tsp ground mace
¼ tsp cumin seeds, dry-roasted (see page 78) and ground
¼ tsp powdered saffron or ½ tsp saffron strands, crushed
3 tbsp chopped cilantro

Place the garlic, preserved lemons, and ginger in a food processor and process to a smooth purée. Add the rest of the ingredients and process. Massage the paste into the meat and allow to marinate in the refrigerator.

HERB RUB

Use herbs such as rosemary, thyme, sage, and oregano to rub into lamb chops, chicken pieces, or game pieces for delicious results.

Enough for about 2–3lb (1–1.5kg) meat

Marinating time: 4–24 hours

Shelf life: 3 months in an airtight container (but use dried instead of fresh herbs and add the garlic just before use)

3 cups (100g) mixture of fresh herbs such as rosemary, thyme, sage, and oregano, finely chopped, or 4 tbsp mixed dried herbs
4 garlic cloves, crushed
1 tbsp salt
grated peel of 1 lemon
1 tbsp coarsely ground black peppercorns
1 tbsp coarsely ground white peppercorns
1 tsp finely ground allspice
1 tbsp mustard powder

Combine all the ingredients in a shallow dish. Dip each piece of meat into the mixture so that it is well coated; then cover and marinate in the refrigerator before frying, broiling, or barbecuing.

TRADITIONAL RIB RUB

¾ cup (150g) dark brown sugar
2 tbsp salt
4 tbsp sweet paprika
3 tbsp coarsely ground or crushed black peppercorns
2 tbsp mustard powder
2 tsp chili powder
2 garlic cloves, crushed

Essential for barbecued or smoked ribs, but also delicious with barbecued chicken.

Enough for 4lb (2kg) ribs or two 3lb (1.5kg) chickens

Marinating time: 24–48 hours

Shelf life: up to 3 days in the refrigerator

Mix all the ingredients together. Massage the mixture into the meat, completely coating it. Cover and let it marinate in the refrigerator.

INDIAN DRY RUB

4 tbsp gram (chickpea) flour
2 tbsp fennel seeds, dry-roasted (see page 78)
2 tbsp coriander seeds, dry-roasted (see page 78)
1 tbsp cumin seeds, dry-roasted (see page 78)
1 tsp cardamom pods, dry–roasted (see page 78)
1 tbsp freshly ground black pepper
2 tsp ground turmeric
½–1 tsp chili powder
¼ tsp asafoetida (optional)

This fragrant and spicy rub is especially good with chicken or fish. The fennel, coriander seeds, cumin, and cardamom pods can be dry-roasted together.

Enough for about 1lb (500g) meat or fish

Marinating time: 6–24 hours

Shelf life: 3 months in an airtight container

1 Put all the ingredients into a blender and process to a fine powder.

2 Transfer the powder to a shallow dish; then dip the meat or fish into it so that it is evenly coated in the mixture. Cover and allow to marinate in the refrigerator, then fry, broil, or barbecue.

SIDE SAUCES

FRUITY, PIQUANT, OR SPICY, SIDE SAUCES ADD TANTALIZING INTEREST TO THE SIMPLEST MEAL. HERE,

I HAVE INCLUDED AN INTERNATIONAL COLLECTION OF MY FAVORITES. PREPARE LARGER QUANTITIES AND PACK

INTO JARS — THEY MAKE CONVENIENT CUPBOARD STAND-BYS AS WELL AS ATTRACTIVE, DELICIOUS GIFTS.

APPLE SAUCE

This delicious sauce is the traditional accompaniment to roast pork; it is perfect with potato pancakes and also makes a wonderful accompaniment to gingerbread. For extra richness, add 2–3 tablespoons of sour cream or crème fraîche.

Serves 6–8

Shelf life: 1 week in the refrigerator; 6 months in a sealed jar (see pages 134–35)

1lb (500g) cooking apples, such as Granny Smith, peeled, cored, and roughly chopped

2–3 tbsp white or brown sugar or honey, or more to taste

1–2 tbsp white wine or water

3–4 cloves

2 inches (5cm) cinnamon stick

2–3 strips of lemon or orange peel

2 tbsp (30g) butter

2–3 tbsp sour cream or crème fraîche (optional)

salt

1 Put the apples, sugar or honey, and white wine or water in a pan. Add the cloves, cinnamon, and lemon or orange peel and bring to a boil. Reduce the heat; cover and cook gently until the apples are soft and beginning to disintegrate, about 10–15 minutes. Remove from the heat. Discard the cloves, cinnamon stick, and lemon or orange peel.

2 Transfer to a blender or food processor, or use an electric mixer or wooden spoon to beat the mixture to a smooth purée. Return to the heat, season with a little salt, then beat in the butter and sour cream or crème fraîche, if using.

CRANBERRY SAUCE

2 cups (250g) fresh or frozen cranberries

juice and grated peel of 1 orange

⅓ cup (100ml) water

1 large cooking apple, such as Granny Smith, peeled, cored, and coarsely grated

½ cup (125g) light brown sugar

¼ cup (60ml) Grand Marnier or other orange liqueur

1 tsp coriander seeds, dry-roasted (see page 78) and coarsely crushed

coarsely ground black pepper

This fragrant, bitter-sweet sauce is a must for roast turkey but also goes very well with cold roast pork and lamb.

Serves 6–8

Shelf life: 1 week in the refrigerator; 6 months in a sealed jar (see pages 134–35)

1 Put the cranberries, orange juice and peel, water, apple, and sugar in a pan and bring to a boil slowly. Reduce the heat and simmer gently until the apple and cranberries are soft and beginning to disintegrate, about 12–15 minutes.

2 Remove from the heat and stir in the Grand Marnier and coriander seeds; then season with black pepper. Set aside to cool before serving.

OPPOSITE: CRANBERRY SAUCE SIMMERING IN THE EARLY STAGES OF COOKING

GOOSEBERRY SAUCE

Tart, refreshing, and pale green in color, this sauce is especially good with fatty fish such as mackerel, herring, or sardines. I also serve it with pork, goose, and duck.

Serves 6–8

Shelf life: 1 week in the refrigerator; 6 months in a sealed jar (see pages 134–35)

1lb (500g) gooseberries, ends trimmed
3 tbsp water
1–2 tbsp sugar, or more to taste
2 tbsp (30g) butter
a pinch of nutmeg (optional)
salt

1 Put the gooseberries, water, and sugar in a pan; bring to a boil and simmer until soft and tender, about 15 minutes. Process to a smooth purée in a food processor or blender; alternatively, press through a strainer.

2 Return the mixture to a clean pan and bring to a boil; then add the butter, stirring until it has melted and been mixed in. Season with the nutmeg, if using, and salt.

VARIATION

PLUM OR CHERRY SAUCE *See page 21 for illustration*
Both sauces make a refreshing accompaniment to ham. Follow the recipe above, but substitute 1lb (500g) pitted plums or cherries for the gooseberries and use ⅓ cup (100ml) white wine or water. Simmer for about 20 minutes, until soft and tender; then purée in a food processor or blender until smooth. Finish by stirring in a pinch of cinnamon.

FRESH BERRY SAUCE

This takes no time at all to prepare and makes a delightful, fruity, yet spicy accompaniment to fish or chicken.

Serves 6–8

Shelf life: 3 days in the refrigerator

2½ cups (300g) fresh berries, such as raspberries, blackberries, strawberries, or blueberries, coarsely chopped
4 scallions, finely chopped
1 tsp green peppercorns in brine, coarsely chopped
2 tbsp raspberry or other berry-flavored vinegar
1–2 tbsp sugar, or to taste
1–2 tbsp chopped fresh tarragon or chervil
salt

Mix all the ingredients together in a bowl and set aside to marinate for at least 1 hour before serving.

CUMBERLAND SAUCE

very thinly pared peel of 1 orange, cut into fine julienne
very thinly pared peel of 1 lemon, cut into fine julienne
¾ cup (250g) redcurrant jelly
4 tbsp port
strained juice of 1 orange
strained juice of 1 lemon
3 tbsp (50g) shallots, chopped (optional)
a pinch of ground ginger
a pinch of cayenne pepper

1 Blanch the orange and lemon peel in boiling water for 1 minute; then drain, refresh in cold water, and drain again well.

2 In a small pan, melt the jelly over a gentle heat; then add the port and simmer for about 3 minutes. Remove from the heat and stir in the blanched peel, the orange and lemon juice, the shallots, if using, and the ginger and cayenne pepper. Set aside to cool before serving.

This sauce is traditionally served with cold ham, pork, or lamb. I like to add chopped raw shallots (an 18th-century idea), which give a marvelous texture and flavor.

Serves 6–8

Shelf life: 1 week in the refrigerator (without the shallots)

VARIATION

CHERRY CUMBERLAND SAUCE
This is excellent with duck, pork, or venison. Follow the recipe above from step 2, omitting the orange and lemon peel and the juice. Instead, add 1¼ cups (250g) chopped fresh or canned sour cherries to the redcurrant jelly while it heats, and stir in 1 teaspoon English mustard with the shallots, if using, and the ginger and cayenne pepper.

MINT SAUCE

5–10 cups (100–150g) fresh mint leaves
1 tbsp sugar
3–4 tbsp white or red wine vinegar

Put the mint leaves on a chopping board, sprinkle the sugar over them, and chop finely. Alternatively, process the mint and sugar in a food processor until finely chopped but not puréed. Transfer the chopped mint to a small bowl and mix with the vinegar.

Mint sauce made with fresh mint is easy to prepare and far superior to the excessively sweet commercial alternative. Serve with lamb or mutton.

Serves 6–8

Shelf life: 1 week in the refrigerator; 6 months in a sealed jar (see pages 134–35)

BREAD SAUCE

This is an adaptation of a 17th-century recipe, although bread sauce is medieval in origin. Mild and delicately flavored, it is traditionally served with roast game, poultry, or pork. Bread sauce should be like cooked oatmeal in consistency, but if you prefer a thinner sauce, dilute it with a little milk or cream. For a more intense flavor, don't discard the onion used to flavor the milk – process it or push it through a strainer and add it to the sauce at the end.

Serves 6–8

Shelf life: 1 week in the refrigerator

1 small onion, peeled and quartered
4 cloves
1 small blade of mace
1 bay leaf
1½ cups (350ml) milk
1½ cups (90g) fresh breadcrumbs
3 tbsp heavy cream
freshly ground nutmeg to taste
2 tbsp (30g) butter
salt and freshly ground black pepper

1 Stud each of the onion quarters with a clove and add to the milk in a small pan along with the mace and bay leaf. Bring to a boil; then reduce the heat and simmer for about 20 minutes.

2 Strain into the top of a double boiler or into a bowl placed over a pan of just-simmering water, making sure the bottom of the bowl does not touch the water.

3 Sprinkle in the breadcrumbs and stir in the cream; then simmer until the sauce is smooth and thick, about 30 minutes.

4 Season with nutmeg and salt and pepper, then beat in the butter and serve hot.

HORSERADISH CREAM SAUCE

6 tbsp (125g) fresh horseradish, peeled and finely grated, or prepared frozen or preserved horseradish
3 tbsp cider vinegar or white wine vinegar
1 tbsp sugar
100ml (3½fl oz) heavy cream
salt

Mix all the ingredients together in a bowl. The horseradish can be preserved in sterilized jars, if desired (see pages 134–35). Fresh horseradish can be very potent – when you work with it, always make sure the room is well ventilated.

I love fresh horseradish sauce with its unique heat and head-clearing qualities. It is traditionally served with roast beef, but I also serve it with cold meats, as a dip for vegetables, and as a sandwich filling.

Serves 6–8

Shelf life: 1 week in the refrigerator; 6 months in a sealed jar (see pages 134–35), but some of its potency will be lost

CHRAIN (HORSERADISH & BEET SAUCE)

5 tbsp (100g) fresh horseradish, peeled and finely grated, or prepared frozen or preserved horseradish
⅛ cup (150g) beets, raw or cooked, peeled and finely grated
3 tbsp distilled vinegar or wine vinegar
1–2 tbsp sugar
salt

Mix all the ingredients together in a bowl. The sauce can be preserved in sterilized jars, if desired.

Chrain, a variant of horseradish sauce, is traditionally served with fish. The beets lend it a vibrant purple color and a sharper flavor.

Serves 6–8

Shelf life: 3 weeks in the refrigerator; 6 months in a sealed jar (see pages 134–35), but some of its potency will be lost

CUMBERLAND SAUCE

MINT SAUCE

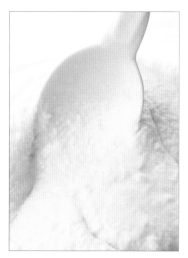

BREAD SAUCE

CHRAIN

PESTO ▷

An herb paste traditionally made from basil, pesto is usually served with pasta but can also be poured over fish or meat before or after broiling. Try it spread over crostini, too, or added to stews, sauces, and soups for extra flavor. For a more intense flavor and the best texture, make pesto with a mortar and pestle.

Shelf life: 1 week in the refrigerator (make sure there is a protective layer of oil over the pesto), although it tastes best eaten immediately

2 large garlic cloves, halved and crushed with the flat side of a large knife

½ tsp coarse salt

½ cup (60g) pine nuts, dry-roasted until golden brown (see page 78)

4 cups (125g) fresh basil leaves

⅔ cup (60g) Parmesan or Pecorino cheese, freshly grated

½ cup (125ml) extra-virgin olive oil

BY HAND: (shown opposite)
1 Put the garlic and salt in a heavy mortar and work to a paste with the pestle.

2 Add the roasted pine nuts and continue pounding and mixing until smooth.

3 Start adding the basil, a small handful at a time; pound and mix until smooth. Sprinkle in the cheese and mix well.

4 Slowly pour in the olive oil in a steady stream and mix until it has a paste-like consistency. Add a little more salt to taste, if necessary, and either serve immediately or transfer to a sterilized container (see pages 134–35).

MACHINE METHOD: put the garlic, salt, roasted pine nuts, basil, and a few tablespoons of the oil in a food processor and process to a paste. Add the cheese and, with the machine running, slowly pour in the remaining oil in a thin, steady stream.

VARIATION

CILANTRO PESTO
This is a refreshing and piquant take on traditional pesto. Serve it as a dip for vegetables, savory pastries, or toasted pita bread. It is delicious in sandwiches but can also be served in the same way as traditional pesto, with pasta or noodles. Like basil pesto, cilantro pesto can be made with a mortar and pestle or in a food processor. Follow the recipe above but substitute ⅓ cup (60g) dry-roasted pistachio nuts for the pine nuts, and instead of basil, use the same amount of cilantro – stems and roots included.

DILL PESTO

2 large garlic cloves, halved and crushed with the flat side of a large knife

2 anchovy fillets in oil, drained and chopped

⅓ cup (75g) pistachio nuts, dry-roasted until lightly browned (see page 78)

6 cups (125g) fresh dill, tough stems removed

⅓ cup (75ml) extra-virgin olive oil

coarsely ground black pepper

BY HAND: pound the garlic and anchovies in a mortar; then add the roasted pistachio nuts and pound to a paste. Continue pounding and mashing; add the dill a little at a time. Pour in the olive oil in a steady stream, mixing until a smooth paste is formed. Season with black pepper.

MACHINE METHOD: process the garlic, anchovies, nuts, dill, and 1 tablespoon of the olive oil until a rough purée is formed. With the machine running, add the remaining olive oil in a thin, steady stream. Season with black pepper.

This is especially good with fish – try drizzling it over smoked salmon canapés.

Shelf life: 1 week in the refrigerator (make sure there is a protective layer of oil over the pesto), although it tastes best eaten immediately

See page 11 for illustration

OLIVE PESTO

4 large garlic cloves, halved and crushed with the flat side of a large knife

3 tbsp chopped fresh thyme

1 large bunch of fresh flat-leaf parsley, tough stems removed

1 cup (100g) black olives, pitted

⅓ cup (75ml) extra-virgin olive oil

BY HAND: pound the garlic and thyme in a mortar; then, mashing and pounding, add the parsley a handful at a time. Add the olives, and pound to a rough purée. Add the olive oil slowly, pounding until a paste is achieved.

MACHINE METHOD: process the garlic, thyme, parsley, olives, and 1 tablespoon of the olive oil until a rough paste. With the machine running, add the rest of the olive oil in a thin, steady stream until the paste is smooth.

For this recipe use sun-dried Mediterranean olives.

Shelf life: 1 week in the refrigerator (make sure there is a protective layer of oil over the pesto), although it tastes best eaten immediately

OPPOSITE: STEPS 1 TO 4 OF MAKING PESTO BY HAND WITH A MORTAR AND PESTLE

TAPENADE

This delicious sauce encapsulates the flavors of the Mediterranean. Originating in the south of France, its name comes from the old Provençal word for capers, tapéno. Traditionally, the sauce is made with a mortar and pestle, which is not particularly time-consuming but can be strenuous work. Serve this versatile sauce as a dip with raw vegetables, spread on crusty bread, or, with plenty of fresh herbs mixed in, as a quick pasta sauce.

Serves 6–8

Shelf life: *1 month in the refrigerator (make sure there is a protective layer of oil over the tapenade)*

1¾oz (50g) anchovy fillets in oil, drained and chopped

2 heaping tbsp capers in vinegar, drained

2 cups (250g) black olives, pitted

4–6 tbsp virgin olive oil

lemon juice to taste

BY HAND: pound the anchovies and capers to a paste in a heavy mortar. Add the olives a few at a time and pound until completely crushed. Start adding the olive oil a little at a time, as if making mayonnaise, and pound until all the oil is used and the mixture is homogeneous. Add the lemon juice and mix well.

MACHINE METHOD: process the anchovies, capers, and olives for a few seconds until roughly chopped but not puréed. With the machine running, pour in the oil in a thin, steady stream. Mix in the lemon juice.

ANCHOÏADE

Traditionally spread on bread and browned in an oven, this southern French paste can be served as a sauce for broiled fish or meat, or just mixed with pasta. Use anchovy fillets preserved in oil or whole, salt-preserved anchovies.

Serves 6–8

Shelf life: *1 month in the refrigerator (make sure there is a protective layer of oil over the anchoïade)*

7oz (200g) anchovy fillets in oil, drained and chopped, or salt-preserved anchovy fillets, soaked in water for 20 minutes, then rinsed and chopped

3 tbsp extra-virgin olive oil

½ cup (100g) shallots, finely chopped

2–3 tbsp lemon juice

a few gratings of lemon peel

6 tbsp chopped fresh flat-leaf parsley

Pound the anchovies to a smooth paste in a mortar, or process in a food processor. Gradually mix in the olive oil; then add the rest of the ingredients and mix well.

SIMPLE SALSA VERDE

2 slices (50g) white bread, torn into small pieces

4 tbsp wine vinegar or lemon juice

5–6 tbsp extra-virgin olive oil

2 tbsp capers in vinegar, drained, or 4 anchovy fillets in oil, drained and chopped

8 tbsp chopped fresh mixed herbs, such as flat-leaf parsley, mint, and basil

1 tbsp sugar

salt and freshly ground black pepper

Mix all the ingredients together in a bowl and set aside to stand for about 1 hour before serving.

VARIATION

AGRODOLCE (SWEET & SOUR SALSA VERDE)
Follow the recipe above but omit the sugar and add 3 tbsp (100g) chopped raisins.

A classic northern Italian sauce, salsa verde, or green sauce, makes a delicious, sharp, and refreshing accompaniment to grilled cheese, meat, poultry, or fish. For a smoother texture, use breadcrumbs instead of bread.

Serves 6–8

Shelf life: *1 month in the refrigerator (make sure there is a protective layer of oil over the salsa verde)*

SKORDALIA

¾lb (300g) starchy potatoes, washed

8–10 garlic cloves, crushed

lemon juice or vinegar to taste

⅔–1 cup (150–250ml) olive oil

salt and freshly ground black pepper

1 Boil the potatoes in their skins until tender. Drain and allow to cool; then rub off the skins and cut the potatoes into chunks.

2 Put the potato pieces into a food processor and process to a smooth paste. Add the garlic and lemon juice or vinegar; then, with the machine running, add the oil in a thin, steady stream until the mixture reaches the consistency of soft mashed potatoes.

3 Season to taste with salt and pepper, then set aside for at least 30 minutes to allow the flavors to develop.

A superbly garlicky sauce of Greek origin, this is traditionally served as part of a mezze. It makes a delicious dip with raw vegetables but can also be served with broiled fish or poultry. Skordalia can be made with bread instead of potatoes: soak 10 slices (300g) white bread, crusts removed, in cold water, then squeeze dry.

Serves 6–8

Shelf life: *3 days in the refrigerator*

ROMESCO ▷

This Spanish sauce gets its name from the romesco peppers that are traditionally used to make it. Serve as a dip or as a sauce for chicken, meat, or fish. If romesco or other dried peppers are not available, use 3 fresh red peppers, roasted and peeled (see page 96), and a little chili powder.

Shelf life: 1 week in the refrigerator; 6 months in a sealed jar (see pages 134–35)

3 plum tomatoes
4 garlic cloves, unpeeled
3 dried romesco peppers or other dried sweet peppers, stems removed, seeded, and soaked in hot water for 30 minutes
½ cup (75g) blanched almonds, dry-roasted until golden (see page 78)
3 tbsp white or red wine vinegar
⅔ cup (150ml) extra-virgin olive oil
salt and freshly ground black pepper

1 Place the tomatoes and garlic in a roasting pan and roast in an oven preheated to 425°F/220°C for about 15 minutes or until soft. Set aside until cool; then peel the tomatoes and squeeze the softened garlic from its papery skin.

2 Drain and coarsely chop the peppers and process in a blender or food processor with the garlic and almonds, or pound in a mortar. Add the tomatoes and vinegar and process or pound to a purée.

3 Add the olive oil in a thin, steady stream and blend until smooth. Season to taste.

ROUILLE

A classic French condiment traditionally served with bouillabaisse or other fish soups. I use it at the table to add piquancy and a garlic flavor to many dishes. If you prefer a thicker consistency, reduce the amount of stock or omit it altogether.

Shelf life: 1 week in the refrigerator; 6 months in a sealed jar (see pages 134–35)

4 large garlic cloves, peeled
2 red peppers, roasted, peeled, and seeded (see page 96), or canned red pimentos
2–4 red chilies, roasted, peeled, and seeded (see page 96)
1 cup (60g) fresh breadcrumbs
3 tbsp olive oil
3 tbsp Fish or Chicken Stock (see pages 30 and 28) (optional)

Process the garlic, red peppers, and chilies in a food processor, or pound in a mortar. Mix in the breadcrumbs and olive oil; then add the fish or chicken stock, if using.

RIGHT: ROMESCO BEING PROCESSED UNTIL SMOOTH

TARATOR

This is part of a large family of ancient Middle Eastern sauces that have nut purées as a base. Serve it as a side sauce with chicken, fish, meat, or vegetables, or as a dip. Tarator can be made with pine nuts, hazelnuts, or almonds instead of walnuts, but be sure to roast the nuts lightly first to enhance their flavor.

Shelf life: *1 week in the refrigerator*

2 garlic cloves, peeled
1 cup (125g) fresh walnuts, lightly dry-roasted (see page 78)
2 slices of white bread, crusts removed, soaked in cold water and squeezed dry
strained juice of ½ lemon
½ cup (100ml) olive oil or Chicken Stock (see page 28)
salt

Process the garlic, walnuts, bread, and lemon juice in a food processor. With the machine running, slowly pour in the oil or stock and process until smooth. Season with salt. Alternatively, use a mortar and pestle to pound the ingredients.

VARIATION

PISTACHIO TARATOR
Use pistachios instead of walnuts, and flavor with ½ teaspoon ground cardamom and 3 tablespoons chopped fresh mint. Serve with lamb.

MUHAMMRA

A hot and piquant Middle Eastern sauce of Syrian origin. Serve as part of a mezze, as a dip with toasted pita bread, or to accompany savory pastries or fritters.

Shelf life: *2 weeks in the refrigerator; 6 months in a sealed jar (see pages 134–35)*

1¼ cups (150g) walnuts, lightly dry-roasted (see page 78)
½ cup (125ml) extra-virgin olive oil
3–5 red chilies, roasted, peeled, and seeded (see page 96), or 1–2 tbsp chili powder moistened with 1 tbsp water
5 red peppers, roasted, peeled, and seeded (see page 96)
1–2 slices of dry white bread, crumbled, or 2–4 tbsp dry white breadcrumbs
3–4 tbsp molasses or 4 tbsp lemon or lime juice and 1 tsp dark sugar
1 tsp ground cumin
1 tsp ground allspice or ½ tsp ground cloves
salt

Process the walnuts and 2 tablespoons of the oil in a food processor until a coarse purée forms. Add the chilies and peppers; mix until roughly chopped. Transfer to a bowl and mix in the rest of the ingredients.

MALAY PEANUT SAUCE

1 onion, peeled
1 inch (2.5cm) piece galangal
2 lemongrass stalks, hard outer layers removed
1 inch (2.5cm) piece ginger
2–4 fresh or dried red chilies, seeded
4 tbsp peanut oil
2½oz (75g) tamarind pulp, soaked in 1 cup (250ml) hot water, then strained (see below)
2–3 tbsp palm sugar or light brown sugar
2 cups (250g) peanuts, roasted, skinned, and coarsely ground, or 1 cup (250g) coarse peanut butter
2–3 tbsp Thai fish sauce (*nam pla*), or salt to taste

A wonderfully fragrant sauce that is traditionally served with satay, but I also like it with broiled meat or fish or as a dip (hot or cold) for raw or steamed vegetables. If galangal is not available, use twice the amount of ginger. Use a crunchy peanut butter that is preferably salt- and sugar-free.

Shelf life: *1 week in the refrigerator*

1 Put the onion, galangal, lemongrass, ginger, and chilies in a food processor and process to a smooth paste.

2 Heat the oil in a pan; then add the paste and sauté, stirring and scraping, for about 10 minutes, until fragrant and nicely browned. Add the tamarind water and bring to a boil. Simmer for about 10 minutes; then add the remaining ingredients and simmer until the sauce has thickened, about 5–10 minutes. Serve warm.

MAKING TAMARIND WATER

1 Pour boiling water over the tamarind pulp in a bowl and mix well. Let it soak for 15–20 minutes, mixing and mashing with a fork from time to time.

2 Pour the mixture into a strainer set over a bowl, pushing through as much of the pulp as possible. Discard the seeds and pulp.

HOT ANCHOVY BUTTER

A hot and garlicky dipping sauce for shrimp or steamed vegetables.

Advance preparation: the garlic butter can be made in advance

Shelf life: 1 week in the refrigerator; 3 months in the freezer

1 recipe Garlic Butter (see page 75)
1¾oz (50g) anchovy fillets in oil, drained and finely chopped
strained juice of 1 lemon
a few scrapings of lemon peel
salt, if necessary, and freshly ground black pepper

Place all the ingredients in a small pan and heat gently until the butter has melted; be careful not to let it burn. Remove from the heat and keep hot at the table on a burner.

HOT PIRI-PIRI BUTTER

A classic African-Portuguese hot butter sauce traditionally served with shrimp. It is a dipping sauce, so it should be brought to the table in the pan and kept warm on a small burner.

Shelf life: 1 week in the refrigerator; 3 months in the freezer

⅝ cup (150g) unsalted butter
strained juice of 1 lemon
a few scrapings of lemon peel
1–3 or more piri-piri chilies, chopped, or chili powder to taste
1–2 garlic cloves, crushed (optional)
salt

Place all the ingredients in a small pan and heat gently until the butter has melted; be careful not to let it burn. Remove from the heat and serve hot.

TAMARIND DIPPING SAUCE

Tart and fruity, this dipping sauce is delicious with vegetables, meat, chicken, or fish kebabs, or with fried pastries. Tamarind is available as a pulp, a paste, or a smooth molasses, but I find that the pulp gives the best flavor.

See page 13 for illustration

3½oz (100g) tamarind pulp soaked in 1 cup (200ml) hot water, then strained (see left)
5 scallions, finely chopped
1–2 red or green chilies, seeded and finely chopped
1 small bunch of fresh cilantro, chopped

Allow the tamarind water to cool to room temperature. In a small bowl, mix it with the scallions, chilies, and cilantro.

CHINESE DIPPING SAUCE

4 tbsp soy sauce
3 tbsp rice vinegar
1 garlic clove, finely chopped
1 tbsp sugar
½ inch (1cm) piece ginger, finely shredded
2 scallions, finely shredded
2–3 tbsp Chili Oil (see page 71, or use commercial chili oil)

An interesting combination of hot and sweet, this sauce is perfect for dipping dumplings, savory pastries, or fried tofu.

Mix all the ingredients together in a small bowl.

THAI DIPPING SAUCE

2 tbsp dark soy sauce
2–3 tbsp Thai fish sauce (*nam pla*)
3 tbsp rice vinegar
1–2 tsp palm sugar or light brown sugar
1 lemongrass stalk, hard outer layers removed, finely chopped
2 red Thai chilies or fresh red bird's eye chilies, sliced into thin rings
2 kaffir lime leaves, shredded

This is quick and easy to make. It is traditionally served as a dipping sauce for fried savory pastries and pies, but it is also delicious spooned over rice or noodles.

See page 15 for illustration

Mix all the ingredients together in a small bowl.

CLASSIC VIETNAMESE DIPPING SAUCE

3 tbsp Thai fish sauce (*nam pla*)
4 tbsp lime juice
1 tsp grated lime zest
2–3 hot chilies, seeded and finely chopped
2 garlic cloves, crushed
1 small carrot, finely shredded

This sharp and hot sauce is traditionally served with fried foods, but it is also good just poured over sizzling-hot, broiled or barbecued fish or poultry.

Mix all the ingredients together in a small bowl.

DESSERT SAUCES

THESE SWEET CONCOCTIONS PLAY AN IMPORTANT ROLE IN DESSERT-MAKING. POURED OVER CAKES, STEAMED

PUDDINGS, FRUIT TARTS, OR ICE CREAM, THEY ADD MOISTURE, TEXTURE, AND FLAVOR. TRY FLAVORING A

SMOOTH CRÈME ANGLAISE WITH SUBTLE AROMATICS, FRUIT PURÉES, OR LIQUEURS; USING A FROTHY ZABAGLIONE

TO TRANSFORM A SIMPLE FRUIT SALAD; OR DRIZZLING A GLORIOUSLY RICH CHOCOLATE SAUCE OVER

PROFITEROLES. ALL THE FAVORITES ARE HERE, AS WELL AS SOME TANTALIZING NEW CREATIONS.

CRÈME ANGLAISE

Velvety and smooth, crème anglaise, or custard, is the classic dessert sauce and a base for many other sweet sauces and desserts. It can be served warm or chilled, poured over fruit or pudding, or even used as a tart filling. For extra richness, replace half or all the milk with light or heavy cream. Custards can be flavored in a multitude of ways (see right). See page 40 for the Crème Anglaise master recipe.

Shelf life: *3 days in the refrigerator*

2 cups (500ml) milk
1 vanilla bean, sliced in half lengthwise, or 1 tsp vanilla extract
6 egg yolks
3–4 tbsp sugar

1 Infuse the milk: scrape the seeds from the vanilla bean, if using, and add both the seeds and the bean or, alternatively, stir the vanilla extract into the milk in a pan. Bring to a boil.

2 In a bowl, beat the egg yolks and sugar together until the mixture is light and foamy. Still beating, pour in the boiling milk.

3 Either place the bowl over a pan of simmering water, making sure the bottom of the bowl does not touch the water, or transfer the mixture, together with the vanilla bean, if using, to the top of a double boiler. Stir continuously until the sauce is thick enough to coat the back of a spoon, about 10–15 minutes. Do not allow the custard to boil. Remove the vanilla bean, if using, then mix well.

VARIATIONS

CHOCOLATE CUSTARD *See page 19 for illustration*
Melt 3oz (90g) dark chocolate in a bowl set over a pan of simmering water. When the Crème Anglaise has cooled a little, stir in the melted chocolate and 2 tablespoons chocolate liqueur.

BRANDY CUSTARD
Let the Crème Anglaise cool a little, then stir in 2–3 tablespoons of brandy or Cognac. Alternatively, use rum or gin to flavor the custard.

BERRY CUSTARD ▷
Set the Crème Anglaise aside to cool a little. Purée ³/₄–1 cup (75–100g) fresh berries of your choice, such as raspberries, blueberries or blackberries, and stir into the custard with sugar to taste. Stir in an appropriate liqueur, if desired.

HONEY CUSTARD
Instead of infusing the milk with vanilla, add 1 small piece of cinnamon stick, 1–2 bay leaves, and 3–4 tablespoons honey.

CARAMEL CUSTARD
Reduce the amount of sugar to 2 tablespoons and add 3–4 tablespoons crushed dark caramel (see page 41) to the milk along with the vanilla.

OPPOSITE: STIRRING FRESH RASPBERRY PURÉE INTO CRÈME ANGLAISE

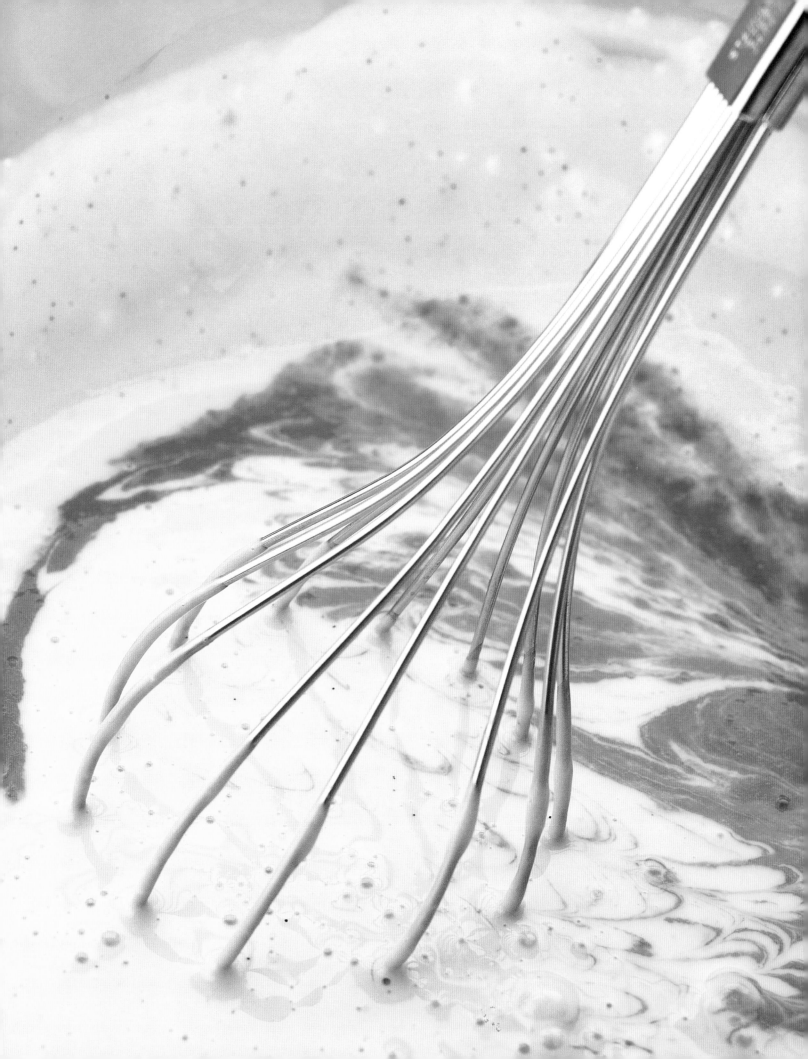

SUGAR SYRUP

This sparkling clear liquid is the sweet equivalent of savory stocks. Use it to dilute fruit coulis, for cooking fruit, to moisten sponge cakes, or as a base for fruit ices and sorbets. Saving sugar syrup causes it to crystallize but adding liquid glucose prevents this from happening.

Shelf life: 3 weeks in the refrigerator

2 cups (500g) sugar
2 cups (450ml) water
1¾oz (50g) liquid glucose (optional)

1 Put the sugar, water, and glucose, if using, in a pan and heat gently, stirring continuously to dissolve the sugar. When all the sugar has dissolved (undissolved sugar will cause crystallization), increase the heat and bring the mixture to a boil.

2 Boil for 2–3 minutes or until the mixture is clear, skimming foam from the surface, if necessary. If the syrup is too thin, boil until the right consistency is achieved; then remove it from the heat.

3 The syrup is ready to use but can also be infused with flavor following one of the three methods below.

VARIATIONS

AROMATICS
Use this method for flavorings such as cloves, cinnamon sticks, allspice, vanilla beans, or cardamom. Add about 1 tablespoon of the crushed aromatic of your choice to the finished sugar syrup and simmer for about 15 minutes. Set aside to cool; then filter (see page 135).

CITRUS PEELS & FLOWERS
Maceration is the most suitable method for flavoring with lemon or orange peel or lavender flowers: place 60–75g (2–2½oz) of the peel or flowers in a sterilized jar (see page 134) and pour over the hot sugar syrup. Set aside to cool, then filter (see page 135).

FLOWER WATERS, ESSENCES, & LIQUEURS
Use this method for flavoring with a flower water such as orange or rose; vanilla or almond extract; rum, kirsch, brandy, or any flavored liqueurs. Set the sugar syrup aside to cool; then stir in 2–3 tablespoons (or more to taste) of the flavoring of your choice.

ZABAGLIONE

4 egg yolks
3 tbsp (50g) sugar
2–3 drops of natural vanilla extract
peel of ½ lemon or orange (optional)
⅖ cup (100ml) marsala, or any strong-flavored sweet white wine

1 Place the egg yolks and sugar in a large bowl and beat either by hand or with an electric mixer until the mixture becomes a pale lemon color. Add the vanilla extract, lemon or orange peel, if using, and marsala and beat until well mixed.

2 Place the bowl over a pan of barely-simmering water, making sure the bottom of the bowl does not touch the water, and beat until the sauce is thick and frothy, about 10–12 minutes. Serve immediately.

3 To serve zabaglione cold, put the bowl in a larger bowl filled with ice and beat gently until it is cold.

The crowning glory of the Italian dessert table, this frothy, velvet-smooth sauce is extremely versatile. Served warm, it makes a glorious sauce for fruit tarts and salads; poured into elegant glasses, it can be served with crisp biscuits as a warm dessert. It can also be eaten cold or frozen as an ice cream-like dessert. To make a lighter version, use only 2 egg yolks and 1 whole egg.

Shelf life: 1 month in the freezer

VARIATION

BLUEBERRY OR MANGO ZABAGLIONE
In a small pan simmer ¾ cup (100g) fresh blueberries or cubed fresh mango with 3–4 tablespoons water or wine until soft. Purée the fruit in a food processor or blender until smooth. Pour the mixture into a strainer, using the back of a spoon to push the mixture through. Stir the fruit purée into the finished zabaglione and serve.

YOGURT & HONEY SAUCE

1 cup (250ml) yogurt, well chilled
1–2 tbsp chopped fresh mint
3 tbsp fragrant clear honey

Place the yogurt in a bowl and stir in the mint. Drizzle the honey on top and fold in very carefully to achieve a marbled effect. Using very cold yogurt will improve the marbled effect.

A startlingly simple yet delicious sauce, this is best served very cold, spooned over hot pancakes, steamed puddings, or fresh fruit. For an extra-rich sauce use thick heavy cream or crème fraîche instead of yogurt.

See page 19 for illustration

BANANA CARAMEL SAUCE

A rich, luscious, and very delicious sauce. Serve hot or cold, with ice cream or flans, or poured over waffles or pancakes. A halved and scraped vanilla bean can be used instead of the cinnamon.

3 ripe bananas, peeled and sliced

a few gratings of lemon peel

strained juice of 1 lemon

¼ cup (60g) butter

4 tbsp soft dark brown sugar

1 tsp ground cinnamon

1 cup (250ml) light cream

2–3 tbsp rum

1 Put the bananas and lemon peel in a bowl; add the lemon juice and mix to coat the bananas in the juice.

2 Melt the butter in a pan; add the sugar and heat gently, stirring constantly, until all the sugar has dissolved.

3 Add the bananas in lemon juice and the cinammon and cook for 10–12 minutes, until the bananas are soft and have started to disintegrate.

4 Tip everything into a blender or food processor and process to a smooth purée. Add the cream and process to blend.

5 Either bring back to the boiling point or set aside to cool, refrigerate, and serve cold. Stir in the rum just before serving.

PINEAPPLE & GINGER SAUCE

1 medium pineapple, peeled, cored, and chopped

1 cup (250g) sugar

4 tbsp white wine or fruit juice

½ tsp of almond extract

1 vanilla bean, sliced in half lengthwise

2oz (60g) chopped preserved stem ginger, soaked in 2 tbsp rum or kirsch for 30 minutes

An aromatic, sweet and sour sauce that goes very well with fruit tarts, ice cream, and soufflés. For the best flavor make sure you use a very ripe pineapple. You can substitute mango for the pineapple, in which case use two large mangoes and reduce the sugar to taste.

1 Put all but about ⅓ cup (75g) of the pineapple in a pan; add the sugar, white wine or fruit juice, and almond extract. Scrape the seeds from the vanilla bean and add both the seeds and the bean to the pan. Bring to a boil; then reduce the heat and simmer until the pineapple is tender, about 20 minutes.

2 Remove from the heat and remove the vanilla bean. Transfer the mixture to a blender and process for 1–2 minutes, until smooth.

3 Return the mixture to the pan. Bring it to a boil; then reduce the heat and simmer until the sauce has become slightly thickened.

4 Chop the reserved pineapple finely and stir into the sauce with the ginger and rum or kirsch. Serve hot or cold.

RAISIN SAUCE

Serve this easy sauce with hot or cold fruit tarts.

1¾ cups (400ml) fragrant, fruity white wine such as Gewürztraminer

1 cup (150g) seedless golden raisins, coarsely chopped

strained juice of 1 lemon

1–2 tbsp honey or sugar, or more to taste

⅓ cup (75ml) heavy cream

2 tbsp (30g) unsalted butter, or Brandy Butter (see page 133), chilled and cubed

2 tbsp rum

In a small pan simmer the wine, raisins, lemon juice, and honey or sugar until the raisins are plump, about 20 minutes. Tip into a blender or food processor and process until smooth. Return the mixture to a clean pan; bring to a boil and stir in first the cream and then the butter a little at a time. Finish by mixing in the rum.

ORANGE & RED WINE SAUCE

This deliciously spicy sauce is wonderful poured over flans and tarts and, of course, ice cream. If blood oranges are not available, use 2 large oranges. Serve hot or cold.

Shelf life: 1 month in the refrigerator

strained juice of 4 blood oranges

1 cup (250ml) full-bodied, fruity red wine

4 tbsp brown sugar

1/2 cinnamon stick, 3 cloves, and 4–5 allspice berries tied in a cheesecloth square

thinly pared peel of 1 orange, cut into thin julienne

1 tsp cornstarch, dissolved in 2 tbsp orange juice or red wine

2 tbsp (30g) unsalted butter, or Orange Butter (see page 133), chilled and cubed

1 Put the orange juice, wine, and sugar in a small pan with the spice bag; bring to a boil and simmer until the mixture is reduced by a third, about 15–20 minutes. Remove the spice bag. In a separate pan, blanch the orange peel in boiling water for 1 minute, then drain, refresh in cold water, and drain again.

2 Add the cornstarch to the wine mixture and simmer for a minute until thickened slightly. Beat in the blanched orange peel and the butter, a little at a time.

PASSION FRUIT SAUCE

Tart and fragrant, this sauce is very easy to make. Serve it hot or cold over cakes and flans or to top ice cream, soufflés, or cheesecakes. The passion fruit seeds add texture and visual interest to this wonderful sauce.

Shelf life: 1 week in the refrigerator

1 tsp cornstarch

strained juice of 3 oranges

3–4 tbsp sugar, or more to taste

1/2 tsp grated lemon peel

6 passion fruit, cut in half

2 tbsp (30g) butter, chilled and cubed

1 Dissolve the cornstarch in 2 tablespoons of the orange juice and set aside. Put the remaining orange juice, the sugar, and the lemon peel in a small pan and boil until reduced by half.

2 Scoop the passion fruit pulp and seeds into the pan and bring to a boil again. Boil for about 1 minute, then add the cornstarch and boil for a further minute until thickened slightly. Beat in the butter a little at a time.

MAPLE PECAN SAUCE

1 cup (200ml) maple syrup

1/3 cup (100ml) heavy cream

1 tbsp instant coffee, dissolved in 2 tbsp boiling water

3/4 cup (75g) pecans, lightly toasted, chopped

1–2 tbsp coffee liqueur (optional)

This flavorful sauce depends on the quality of the maple syrup; buy the real thing and avoid artificially flavored substitutes. Serve over ice cream and steamed puddings, or simply poured on hot waffles or pancakes.

1 In a small pan, bring the maple syrup and cream to a boil, then reduce the heat to medium and simmer, stirring frequently, until slightly reduced, about 5 minutes.

2 Remove from the heat and allow to cool a little, then stir in the coffee, the nuts, and the liqueur, if using.

COOKED FRUIT COULIS

2½ cups (300g) soft fruit, such as raspberries, strawberries, or blackberries, or 1lb (500g) fruit, such as cherries or plums, pitted

1¼ cups (400ml) water

1/2–2/3 cup (100–150g) sugar, or to taste

strained juice of 1/2 lemon

1/4 cup (60ml) liqueur (optional)

A simple classic that is extremely versatile and can be served chilled or warm to add moisture and contrasting flavor to any dessert. You could substitute other fruit, such as mangoes, papaya, or pineapple, as long as the amount after pitting and peeling is about 2½ cups (300g). Choose a liqueur that complements the fruit.

Shelf life: 1 week in the refrigerator

1 Place the fruit, water, sugar, and lemon juice in a pan. Bring to a boil, then reduce the heat and simmer for 20–25 minutes or until the fruit is soft and mushy and beginning to disintegrate.

2 Remove from the heat; transfer the mixture to a blender or food processor and process until smooth. Pour the sauce through a fine strainer, stir in the liqueur, if using, and chill.

VARIATION

FRESH FRUIT COULIS
A fresh version of the recipe above, this works best with soft fruit. Put the fruit and liqueur in a food processor with 1 cup (250ml) Sugar Syrup (see page 128). Process until smooth, then pour through a fine strainer and serve chilled.

SIMPLE CHOCOLATE SAUCE

Use the best-quality chocolate you can find, with as high a cocoa solids content as possible – many supermarkets now sell a 70% cocoa solids bar. For a richer sauce, replace the milk with light or heavy cream. Vary the flavor by adding brandy, rum, or flavored liqueurs such as Grand Marnier, mint, or almond, or use flavoring essences such as rose water, orange flower, or vanilla.

Shelf life: *1 week in the refrigerator (reheat gently in a bowl placed over a pan of simmering water)*

7oz (200g) dark chocolate
1/3 cup (75ml) milk
1/3 cup (75ml) heavy or light cream
2–3 tbsp sugar, or to taste

1 Break the chocolate into pieces and put into a bowl placed over a pan of simmering water, making sure the bottom of the bowl does not touch the water. Melt the chocolate, stirring occasionally.

2 Put the milk, cream, and sugar in a pan and bring to a boil. Gently pour the hot milk and cream mixture into the melted chocolate and mix until smooth. Either serve hot or set aside to cool, stirring from time to time to prevent a skin forming.

WHITE CHOCOLATE SAUCE

This is a simple chocolate sauce with a hint of orange. Use with the Simple Chocolate Sauce above to create a striking black and white effect.

Shelf life: *1 week in the refrigerator (reheat gently in a bowl placed over a pan of simmering water)*

7oz (200g) white chocolate, broken into pieces
1 cup (200ml) heavy cream
1/3 cup (75ml) milk
1–2 strips orange peel (optional)

1 Melt the chocolate in a bowl placed over a pan of simmering water, making sure the bottom of the bowl does not touch the water. Stir until smooth.

2 Put the cream, milk, and orange peel, if using, in a small pan and bring to a boil. Reduce the heat and simmer for 2–3 minutes; then remove the orange peel.

3 Gently pour the hot cream and milk mixture into the melted chocolate, stirring constantly until smooth. Serve the sauce warm or set aside to cool and serve at room temperature.

FUDGE SAUCE

1¾ cup (400ml) evaporated milk
⅓ cup (75–100g) sugar
1 vanilla bean, sliced in half lengthwise, or 1 tsp vanilla extract
5oz (150g) dark chocolate, broken into pieces
2 tbsp (30g) unsalted butter
a pinch of salt

This is traditionally served with ice cream but it can also be poured over steamed puddings or served as a tart filling.

Shelf life: *1 month in the refrigerator*

1 Heat the evaporated milk, sugar, and vanilla bean or extract in a pan over a medium heat, stirring to dissolve the sugar. Bring to a rolling boil and boil for 1 minute, stirring constantly.

2 Remove from the heat and remove the vanilla bean, if using. Scrape the seeds from the bean and add them to the milk; discard the bean. Add the chocolate and stir until it has melted. Add the butter and salt and mix until smooth. Serve hot or cold.

VARIATIONS

RICH FUDGE SAUCE
Substitute 1 cup (250ml) heavy cream for the evaporated milk and ⅓ – ½ cup (75–100g) light brown sugar for the white sugar. Omit the vanilla and the salt and stir in ½ teaspoon ground cinnamon.

NUT FUDGE SAUCE
Stir ⅔ cup (75g) chopped, lightly toasted pecans or almonds into Fudge Sauce or Rich Fudge Sauce.

GINGER FUDGE SAUCE
Flavor Fudge Sauce or Rich Fudge Sauce with ½ tsp ground ginger and 1¾oz (50g) chopped candied ginger, rinsed to remove sugared coating.

BRANDY FUDGE SAUCE
Stir 2 tablespoons brandy or rum into the finished Fudge Sauce or Rich Fudge Sauce.

SWEET BUTTERS

Melt sweet butters on hot pancakes, waffles, or puddings or use them as simple fillings or frostings for sponge cakes. I add them where I would normally use plain butter, to give flavor, richness, and gloss to dessert sauces. I don't like my butters too sweet, so I use ¼ cup (75g) sugar to 7 tbsp (100g) butter, but you can increase the sugar to ½ cup (100g) or more if you have a sweet tooth. Sweet butters can be made by hand, but an electric mixer will produce lighter and fluffier results.

BRANDY BUTTER

This famous sweet butter is the traditional accompaniment to plum pudding.

Shelf life: *2 weeks in the refrigerator; 3 months in the freezer*

7 tbsp (100g) unsalted butter, softened
⅓ cup (75g) sugar
2–3 tbsp brandy
a few drops of lemon juice (optional)
½ tsp grated lemon peel (optional)

Cream the butter and sugar together until white and fluffy. Add the brandy, lemon juice, and peel, if using, and beat until well mixed. Place the butter on a piece of waxed paper and roll into a cylinder shape (see page 74). Chill until firm.

VARIATIONS

ORANGE BUTTER
Substitute an orange liqueur such as Cointreau, Grand Marnier, or triple sec for the brandy. Add 1 teaspoon grated orange peel instead of the lemon juice and peel.

CHERRY BUTTER ▷
Substitute cherry brandy, kirsch, or any other cherry liqueur for the brandy and mix in ¼ cup (50g) chopped fresh or glacé cherries. Omit the lemon juice and peel.

RUM & GINGER BUTTER *See page 23 for illustration*
Substitute dark brown sugar for the white sugar (or, for a softer, lighter butter, use light brown sugar). Use rum instead of the brandy and mix in 1oz (30g) chopped candied ginger from which the sugared coating has been rinsed.

Right: Cherry Butter melting on hot waffles

KEEPING & FREEZING

THESE ARE SIMPLE METHODS for extending the shelf-life of certain sauces. You can preserve many of the sauces in this book in sterilized jars in the refrigerator, but any with low acidity or a low sugar or salt content need to be heat processed, especially if you want to store them for longer than three or four months.

STERILIZING JARS

A CONVENIENT AND EFFECTIVE WAY to sterilize jars is to boil them. Once sterilized, the jars are suitable for canning and storing food. Special clamp-top jars are available (always use new rubber rings), but you can also use screw-top jars, many of which have a rubber seal.

Wash the jars thoroughly in hot, soapy water before you begin; then place a cake rack or upturned saucer in the bottom of a large pan to prevent the jars from breaking or cracking. When placing jars in the pan, make sure that they do not touch each other or the sides of the pan during boiling.

After boiling, remove the pan from the heat, lift the jars out with tongs and drain upside down on a clean kitchen towel. Place the jars on a kitchen towel-lined baking tray and dry in a cool oven.

1 Put a cake rack or upturned saucer in the bottom of a pan. Put the jars, lids, and any rubber seals on top; fill with hot water until they are completely immersed and boil rapidly for 10 minutes. Drain, upside down, on a kitchen towel.

2 Dry in a cool oven on a kitchen towel-lined baking pan. Once sterilized, reassemble each jar. Attach the new, sterilized rubber ring, if using, by placing it on the lid of the jar, then stretching and fitting it into place.

HEAT PROCESSING

THE PROCESS OF BOILING and then cooling the filled jars causes the contents to contract and form a vacuum; this seals the food and prevents it from coming into contact with oxygen, thus preserving it.

To boil, wrap each filled jar in a few layers of cloth, such as an old dish towel, or newspaper to prevent the jars from knocking against each other. Place a cake rack or an upturned saucer in the bottom of a large pan to prevent the jars from touching the bottom, and put the jars on top. Fill with water, covering the jars, and checking the water level from time to time; add more water if necessary.

After processing for the recommended time (see chart opposite), remove the pan from the heat and lift the jars out with tongs. Set aside to cool completely; then check the seal (see Tips for Keeping, opposite).

1 Fill the hot, sterilized jars to within ½ inch (1cm) of the top with the hot or cold sauce. Clamp the lid shut. Wrap the jars in cloth (see left) and place in a pan on a cake rack or upturned saucer.

2 Pour in enough hot water to cover the lids of the jars by at least 1 inch (2.5cm). Cover the pan, bring to a boil, and boil for the recommended time (see chart opposite).

HEAT PROCESSING TIMES

All the times are counted from the moment the water comes back to a boil.

Heat processing times for cold-packed preserves

1 pint (1lb) (500g) jars – 25 minutes

2lb (1kg) jars – 30 minutes

1 quart (1 liter) bottles – 30 minutes

Heat processing times for hot-packed preserves

1 pint (1lb) (500g) jars – 20 minutes

2lb (1kg) jars – 25 minutes

1 quart (1 liter) bottles – 25 minutes

TIPS FOR PRESERVING

To test a seal on a clamp-top jar
Gently unclamp the lid and slowly lift the jar holding just the lid – if sealed it will support the weight.

To test a seal on a one-piece lidded jar
Check for a dip in the middle of the lid – this shows that a vacuum has formed.

If a seal has not formed
Pour the contents of the jar into a pan and boil for 3–4 minutes. Return to a clean jar and repeat the sterilizing process.

FILTERING

VINEGARS, OILS, AND OTHER LIQUIDS can become cloudy and need filtering before storage. Filtering also removes flavoring ingredients.

To filter, carefully pour the liquid through a cheesecloth-lined funnel into a clean bottle.

FREEZING

FREEZING IS THE BUSY COOK'S ALTERNATIVE to preserving in jars and is the simplest and most convenient way of extending the storage life of food.

Do not freeze food for longer than recommended in the recipe since this can cause discoloration and may alter the texture and consistency. Label all containers and packages of food; then check the contents of your freezer regularly and discard anything that has outlived its freezing time.

Try to freeze food in convenient quantities – in single portions or in ice cube trays, for example. Freeze only the freshest food in perfect condition. When freezing liquids, leave ½ inch (1cm) space at the top of the container to allow for expansion.

Cool hot food quickly before freezing it; do not be tempted to put warm food in the freezer since this creates condensation.

Making Ice Cubes
Herb purée, tomato paste, and stock can easily be frozen as blocks in ice cube trays. The cubes can then be stored in bags in the freezer and added in convenient quantities to a recipe.

Filling Containers
Choose containers that seal tightly and won't leak. Write the contents and the date on a label and adhere it to the container.

TROUBLESHOOTING

IF YOU ENCOUNTER PROBLEMS with any of your sauces, the chart below should help you to understand why they may have occurred and, in most cases, how to correct what has gone wrong. The chart also includes tips to help you improve the texture, correct the consistency, and enhance the flavor of your sauces.

	PROBLEM	POSSIBLE CAUSE	REMEDY
STOCKS	• Cloudy	• Bones not washed thoroughly; not skimmed well enough; allowed to boil; not allowed to settle	• See Troubleshooting box, page 29
	• Too thin	• Not enough bones; inferior bones; not enough vegetables; not allowed to reduce enough	• Add more bones and vegetables or allow to reduce further
	• Fatty	• Not skimmed well enough	• Chill in the refrigerator and skim well (see page 28)
WHITE SAUCES	• Lumpy	• Not beaten enough; brought to a boil too quickly	• Strain or process in the blender; then return to the pan and heat to boiling point (see Troubleshooting box, page 32)
	• Too thick	• Reduced too much; not enough milk	• Dilute with a little milk or cream
	• Too thin	• Not reduced enough; too much milk	• Add a little beurre manié (see page 45); bring back to a boil and cook until reduced and thickened
CHEESE SAUCE	• Too thick	• Reduced too much; too much flour in the base sauce; too much cheese	• Dilute with a little milk or cream and heat through
	• Too thin	• Too much liquid; not enough cheese	• Add a little more cheese and heat through
	• Lumpy	• Not beaten enough; cheese has not melted properly	• Return to the heat and beat until smooth
	• Stringy	• Cooked too long or on too high a heat; the protein of the cheese has cooked and become stringy	• No remedy
VELOUTÉ	• Too thin	• Not enough flour; too much liquid; not reduced enough	• Either reduce further or add 2–3 teaspoons (15–30g) beurre manié (see page 45) and beat well; bring to a simmer and beat for 3–4 minutes to cook the flour
	• Lumpy	• Not beaten enough	• Pour through a strainer
	• Insipid	• Badly made or flavorless stock; not reduced enough; not enough flavoring	• Adjust seasoning or add some vegetables, reduce further, and strain
HOLLANDAISE	• Too thin	• Too little butter; base reduction not reduced enough	• Add more butter
	• Separated	• Cooked too quickly; butter added too quickly	• See Troubleshooting box, page 34
	• Curdled	• Cooked over too high a heat or for too long	• No remedy
BEURRE BLANC & VARIATIONS	• Too thin	• Base reduction not reduced enough; butter not cold enough; not enough butter; not beaten enough	• Remove from the heat and whisk vigorously
	• Separated	• Butter added too quickly; butter not cold enough; cooked over too high a heat	• Add 2–3 tablespoons heavy cream and bring to a quick boil; reduce for 1–2 minutes, lower the heat, and add the separated sauce a spoonful at a time, beating continuously until the sauce is amalgamated; serve immediately
	• Insipid	• Base reduction not flavorsome enough; poor-quality butter	• Season with a little lemon juice, pepper, and/or chili powder
REDUCTION SAUCES	• Too thin	• Not reduced enough	• Return to the heat and reduce further
	• Too thick	• Reduced too much	• Add a little wine or stock and cook for a further 1–2 minutes
	• Cloudy	• Not skimmed well enough; boiled too quickly in early stages	• Strain through cheesecloth (see Stocks, pages 28–31)
GRAVY	• Too thick	• Too much flour or thickener; reduced too much	• Add a little stock or wine and cook for 1–2 minutes.
	• Too thin	• Not reduced enough; too little flour or thickener	• Either reduce further or add 2 teaspoons or more of beurre manié (see page 45) and cook for 2–3 minutes
	• Lumpy	• Liquid added too quickly; not beaten enough	• Pass through a sieve

	PROBLEM	POSSIBLE CAUSE	REMEDY
VINAIGRETTE	• Separated	• Not beaten enough; left to stand for too long	• Whisk vigorously or start again with 1 teaspoon of mustard and beat in the separated vinaigrette
	• Too thin	• Too little oil, not enough mustard	• Add some mustard or cream
	• Too sour	• Too much vinegar or lemon juice	• Add some sugar or more oil
OILS	• Off-smelling	• Oil exposed to oxygen	• No remedy, discard
	• Cloudy	• Stored at too low a temperature; reaction of oil to ingredients	• Does not affect the flavor, try to remedy by straining through cheesecloth (see page 135)
MAYONNAISE	• Separated	• Oil added too quickly; not beaten enough	• See Troubleshooting box, page 38
	• Too thick	• Too much oil	• Whisk in a little lemon juice, vinegar, water, or cream
	• Too thin	• Not enough oil; too much vinegar or lemon juice	• Whisk in some more oil
COOKING SAUCES	• Too thick	• Cooked too long	• Dilute with an appropriate liquid
	• Too thin	• Too much liquid	• Thicken with beurre manié, cornstarch or arrowroot (see pages 44–45) or boil rapidly to reduce
COOKED TOMATO SAUCES	• Too thick	• Cooked too long	• Dilute with a little wine, stock, or water
	• Too thin	• Not cooked long enough; tomatoes too watery	• Cook further or thicken with cornstarch or arrowroot (see pages 44–45)
	• Bitter or too sour	• Cooked too long; burned; too many herbs and spices; tomatoes too sour	• Sweeten with a little sugar
SALSAS	• Watery	• Vegetables too watery; allowed to stand for too long	• Strain, add breadcrumbs (see page 45) and adjust flavoring
	• Fermented	• Allowed to stand for too long; not enough salt or acidity	• Discard immediately
RELISHES	• Fermented	• Not enough acid or sugar; not cooked enough	• No remedy, discard
	• Mouldy	• Not enough acid or sugar; not cooked enough; stored in an unsterilized container; seal broken	• No remedy, discard
	• Discolored	• Exposed to light	• Does not affect the flavor
CRÈME ANGLAISE	• Curdled	• Cooked too long or over too high a heat causing the egg protein to cook	• See Troubleshooting box, page 40; no remedy if eggs completely coagulated
	• Too thin	• Not cooked for long enough	• Cautiously raise the heat and continue to cook
SUGAR SYRUP	• Cloudy	• Sugar not dissolved properly	• Strain through cheesecloth or clarify with egg as for stock (see Troubleshooting box, page 29)
	• Fermented	• Kept for too long; sugar not concentrated enough	• No remedy, discard
ZABAGLIONE	• Curdled	• Cooked over too high a heat; overworked	• No remedy
	• Too thin	• Too much liquid; not cooked enough	• Cook further while beating or fold in 1 stiffly beaten egg white
FRUIT COULIS	• Too thick	• Not enough sugar syrup or liquid; not processed fine enough	• Dilute with a little sugar syrup or pass through a sieve
	• Too thin	• Not enough fruit; too much sugar syrup	• Add more puréed fruit or thicken with cornstarch or arrowroot (see pages 44–45)
CHOCOLATE SAUCE	• Too thick	• Too much chocolate; too little butter or milk	• Dilute with a little cream or an appropriate liqueur
	• Too thin	• Too little chocolate; not cooked for long enough	• Add some more chocolate; continue to cook
	• Dull	• Poor-quality chocolate; not beaten enough	• Add 1 tablespoon of unflavored oil or butter and beat well
	• Hard and stringy	• Cooked over too high a heat	• No remedy
	• Chocolate seizes	• Chocolate coming into contact with water or steam while melting	• Add a little butter or vegetable oil and stir until smooth again

MATCHING SAUCES WITH FOOD

Use this chart to help you partner sauces with basic ingredients and as an inspirational guide for creating imaginative and delicious meals. Don't stop with these suggestions; experiment with different combinations and enjoy sauces for their tremendous versatility, whether planning a simple meal or an impressive feast.

SAVORY SAUCES

	Poultry	Beef	Pork	Lamb	Fish & shellfish	Vegetables	Salads	Pasta, rice, & noodles
Soubise (p.48)	•			•		•		
Caramelized Soubise (p.48)		•		•		•		
Mushroom Sauce (p.49)	•				•	•		•
Robust Mushroom Sauce (p.49)	•	•				•		•
Mornay Sauce (p.49)					•	•		•
Blue Cheese Sauce (p.49)	•	•				•		•
Béchamel (pp.32–3)						•		•
Exotic Béchamel (p.50)	•				•	•		
Aurora (p.50)	•				•	•		
Parsley Sauce (p.50)	•				•	•		
Mixed Herb Sauce (p.50)	•				•	•		
Velouté (p.52)	•		•		•			
Caper Sauce (p.52)			•	•	•			
Lemongrass & Coconut Sauce (p.52)	•				•	•		
Supreme Sauce (p.53)	•				•	•		
Olive Oil Sauce (p.53)	•				•	•		
Mustard Sauce (p.53)	•		•	•	•	•		
Béarnaise (p.54)		•			•			
Beurre Blanc (p.54)					•			
Orange Butter Sauce (p.54)	•				•			
Lemongrass Butter Sauce (p.54)	•				•			•
Chili Butter Sauce (p.54)	•	•				•		
Hollandaise (pp.34–5)					•	•		
Maltaise (p.55)	•				•			
Exotic Hollandaise (p.55)	•				•			
Sabayon (pp.36–7)					•			
Pink Champagne Sabayon (p.57)					•			
Seafood Sabayon (p.57)					•			
Avgolemono (p.57)	•							
Orange & Saffron Sabayon (p.57)					•			
Watercress Coulis (p.58)					•	•		
Carrot Coulis (p.58)	•					•		
Avocado Coulis (p.59)	•					•		
Fresh Tomato Coulis (p.59)	•					•		•
Cooked Tomato Coulis (p.59)	•	•	•	•	•	•		•
Demi-glaze (p.60)		•						
Madeira Demi-glaze (p.61)		•						
Red Demi-glaze (p.61)		•						
Juniper Demi-glaze (p.61)				•				
Thickened Demi-glaze (p.61)	•	•						
Wild Mushroom Demi-glaze (p.62)	•			•				
Red Wine Sauce (p.62)					•			
Orange & Saffron Sauce (p.62)	•			•				

	Poultry	Beef	Pork	Lamb	Fish & shellfish	Vegetables	Salads	Pasta, rice, & noodles
Ginger & Scallion Sauce (p.64)					•			
Lemon Sauce (p.64)					•			
Balsamic Vinegar Sauce (p.64)	•				•			
Traditional Pan Gravy (p.65)	•	•	•					
Tomato Gravy (p.65)	•	•	•	•				
Mustard Gravy (p.65)	•	•	•					
Gravy for Lamb or Game (p.65)				•				
Onion Gravy (p.65)		•	•					
Caramelized Onion Gravy (p.65)		•	•	•				
Blue Cheese Dressing (p.66)		•					•	
Thousand Island Dressing (p.66)		•					•	
Feta Cheese Dressing (p.66)						•	•	
Mango Dressing (p.66)	•				•	•	•	
Sour Cream Dressing (p.68)					•	•	•	
Tahini Sauce (p.68)						•	•	
Hazelnut Tahini (p.68)						•	•	
Peanut Tahini (p.68)	•					•	•	
Green Tahini (p.68)	•				•	•	•	
Salad Cream (p.68)						•	•	
Vinaigrette (p.68)	•					•	•	
Roquefort Dressing (p.68)		•					•	
Garlic & Herb Vinaigrette (p.68)						•	•	
Pepper & Chili Vinaigrette (p.69)	•					•	•	
Cooked Vinaigrette (p.69)						•	•	
Steve's Spicy Vinaigrette (p.69)						•	•	
Raspberry Vinaigrette (p.69)	•					•	•	
Warm Maple Vinaigrette (p.69)	•					•	•	
Herb Oil (p.70)	•	•			•	•	•	•
Lavender Oil (p.70)	•				•			
Thai Caramelized Oil (p.70)	•					•	•	•
Lemon Oil (p.70)	•				•	•	•	
Garlic Oil (p.70)	•					•	•	•
Fresh Chili Oil (p.71)	•	•	•			•		•
Smoky Chili Oil (p.71)	•	•	•			•		•
Kaffir Lime Oil (p.71)	•				•	•	•	
Mayonnaise (p.72)					•		•	
Garlic Mayonnaise (p.72)					•	•	•	
Herb Mayonnaise (p.72)	•				•		•	
Smoky Red Pepper Mayonnaise (p.72)	•				•	•		
Orange Mustard Mayonnaise (p.72)	•		•		•			
Beet Mayonnaise (p.72)					•		•	
Harissa Mayonnaise (p.72)					•	•	•	
Shrimp Cocktail Sauce (p.72)					•		•	

	Poultry	Beef	Pork	Lamb	Fish & shellfish	Vegetables	Salads	Pasta, rice, & noodles
Green Goddess Dressing (p.72)		•			•		•	
Gribiche (p.73)		•			•			
Tartare Sauce (p.73)					•		•	
Yogurttaise (p.73)					•	•	•	
Aïoli (p.73)	•	•		•	•	•	•	
Rémoulade (p.73)	•	•	•		•		•	
Chili Butter (p.74)	•	•	•	•	•	•		•
Lemongrass & Lime Butter (p.74)	•		•	•	•	•		
Tomato Butter (p.74)	•	•		•	•	•		
Anchovy Butter (p.75)		•			•	•		
Lemon Butter (p.75)	•				•	•		
Garlic Butter (p.75)	•	•	•	•	•	•		
Spicy Tomato & Chili Sauce (p.76)					•	•		
Spicy Tomato & Fennel Sauce (p.76)	•				•			
Spicy Pepper Sauce (p.76)	•	•				•	•	
Dry Curry (p.78)	•	•		•				
Dry Vegetable Curry (p.79)						•		
Anglo-Indian Curry (p.79)	•	•	•			•		
Lamb Korma (p.80)				•				
Chicken Korma (p.80)		•						
Paneer or Tofu Korma (p.80)						•		
Rogan Josh (p.82)		•		•				
Vanilla Curry (p.82)		•						
Sabzi (p.83)	•	•		•				
Plum Sauce for Fish (p.83)					•			
Sweet & Sour Sauce (p.84)		•	•	•				
Fruity Sweet & Sour Sauce (p.84)	•		•					
Black Bean Sauce (p.84)	•	•	•	•		•		
Red Curry Paste (p.85)		•	•	•				
Yellow Curry Paste (p.85)	•			•		•		
Green Curry Paste (p.86)	•	•	•			•		
Light Curry for Fish (p.86)					•			
Mole (p.88)		•		•				
Chili con Carne (p.89)		•		•				
Manchamantel (p.89)		•	•					
Passata (p.90)	•	•	•			•		•
Arrabbiata (p.90)		•						•
Eggplant Sauce (p.90)					•	•		•
Tomato & Tuna Sauce (p.91)								•
Tomato & Broiled Zucchini Sauce (p.91)								•
Vongole (p.92)								•
Three-tomato Sauce (p.92)	•				•	•		•
Wild Mushroom Sauce (p.92)		•						•
Creamy Mushroom Sauce (p.92)	•	•						•
Three-chili Salsa (p.94)	•	•			•	•		•
Tomato & Cucumber Salsa (p.94)	•				•		•	
Tomato & Pepper Salsa (p.96)			•	•	•			
Papaya & Kaffir Lime Salsa (p.96)	•		•		•			
Exotic Papaya & Kaffir Lime Salsa (p.96)	•	•	•		•			
Beet & Apple Salsa (p.96)						•	•	
Tomatillo Salsa (p.97)	•	•	•	•		•	•	
Pomegranate & Herb Salsa (p.97)		•			•	•		
Guacamole (p.97)		•						

	Poultry	Beef	Pork	Lamb	Fish & shellfish	Vegetables	Salads	Pasta, rice, & noodles
Mixed Pepper Salsa (p.98)	•	•			•	•		
Citrus Salsa (p.98)	•				•	•		
Mango & Tomato Salsa (p.98)	•				•		•	•
Roast Corn Salsa (p.98)	•	•	•			•		
Fresh Onion Chutney (p.100)						•	•	
Herb Chutney (p.100)						•	•	
Coconut Chutney (p.100)						•		•
Cashew Nut Chutney (p.100)	•					•		
Green Chili Chutney (p.101)			•	•				
Carrot Chutney (p.101)	•					•		
Banana Chutney (p.101)	•	•	•	•				
Matbucha (p.102)	•							
Green Chili Relish (p.102)		•	•					
Harissa (p.103)	•	•		•	•	•		•
Fruity Chili Relish (p.103)	•					•		
Two-tomato Relish (p.103)	•					•		
Exotic Fruit Relish (p.103)	•					•		
Onion Raita (p.104)						•	•	
Tomato Raita (p.104)	•			•		•	•	•
Quince Sambal (p.104)	•	•	•	•		•		•
Carrot Sambal (p.104)	•	•		•				
Cucumber Sambal (p.104)					•	•		
Smoky Eggplant Dip (p.105)						•	•	
Pepper & Eggplant Dip (p.105)						•		
Feta & Eggplant Dip (p.105)						•	•	
Yogurt, Garlic, & Lemon Dip (p.105)						•	•	
Simple Yogurt Dip (p.105)						•	•	
Bean Dip (p.106)						•		
Pepper Dip (p.106)						•	•	
Taramasalata (p.106)						•	•	
Sour Cream & Saffron Dip (p.106)						•	•	
Fresh Herb Lamb Marinade (p.108)				•				
Mediterranean Fish Marinade (p.108)					•			
Cider & Herb Marinade (p.110)			•	•				
Traditional Barbecue Sauce (p.110)	•	•	•	•				
Barbecue Sauce with Cocoa (p.110)		•	•					
Tandoori Marinade (p.110)	•			•				
Orange & Ginger Sauce (p.111)	•				•			
Beer Marinade (p.111)		•	•					
Ceviche (p.112)					•			
Tzaramelo (p.112)	•				•			
Oriental Soy Marinade (p.113)	•	•			•	•		•
Lemon & Chili Marinade (p.113)	•				•			
Apricot & Herb Marinade (p.113)			•	•				
Chimichurri (p.113)		•		•				
South African Sosatie (p.113)	•	•		•				
Herb Paste for Fish (p.114)							•	
Paste for Cooked Meats (p.114)	•	•	•	•				
Papaya Marinating Paste (p.114)		•		•				
Jamaican Jerk Paste (p.114)	•	•	•					
North African Spice Paste (p.115)	•			•				
Herb Rub (p.115)		•		•				
Traditional Rib Rub (p.115)		•	•					

	Poultry	Beef	Pork	Lamb	Fish & shellfish	Vegetables	Salads	Pasta, rice, & noodles
Indian Dry Rub (p.115)	•	•	•	•	•			
Apple Sauce (p.116)			•			•		
Cranberry Sauce (p.116)	•		•	•				
Gooseberry Sauce (p.118)					•			
Cherry Sauce (p.118)		•	•	•				
Plum Sauce (p.118)	•		•	•	•	•		
Fresh Berry Sauce (p.118)	•			•	•			
Cumberland Sauce (p.118)	•	•		•				
Cherry Cumberland Sauce (p.118)	•	•		•				
Mint Sauce (p.118)				•				
Bread Sauce (p.119)	•							
Horseradish Cream Sauce (p.119)	•	•						
Chrain (p.119)	•				•			
Pesto (p.120)	•				•	•		•
Dill Pesto (p.120)	•							•
Cilantro Pesto (p.120)	•							•
Olive Pesto (p.120)	•				•			•
Tapenade (p.122)					•	•		•
Anchoiade (p.122)					•	•		•
Simple Salsa Verde (p.122)	•		•	•	•			•
Agrodolce (p.122)	•							
Skordalia (p.122)	•							
Romesco (p.123)			•		•			
Rouille (p.123)	•				•			
Tarator (p.124)	•					•		
Pistachio Tarator (p.124)	•					•		
Muhammra (p.124)	•					•		
Malay Peanut Sauce (p.124)	•	•	•	•		•		
Hot Anchovy Butter (p.125)	•					•		
Hot Piri-Piri Butter (p.125)	•					•		
Tamarind Dipping Sauce (p.125)	•				•			
Chinese Dipping Sauce (p.125)	•					•		
Thai Dipping Sauce (p.125)	•	•	•	•	•	•		
Vietnamese Dipping Sauce (p.125)	•	•	•	•		•		

DESSERT SAUCES

	Ice cream	Fruit	Tarts	Steamed puddings	Pancakes
Crème Anglaise (p.126)	•	•	•		
Chocolate Custard (p.126)	•		•		
Brandy Custard (p.126)	•		•	•	
Berry Custard (p.126)	•	•	•		
Honey Custard (p.126)	•	•	•		•
Caramel Custard (p.126)	•	•	•		
Sugar Syrup (p.128)	•	•			•
Zabaglione (p.128)		•	•		
Blueberry Zabaglione (p.128)		•	•		
Mango Zabaglione (p.128)		•			•
Yogurt & Honey Sauce (p.128)		•	•	•	
Banana Caramel Sauce (p.129)	•				
Pineapple & Ginger Sauce (p.129)	•	•			
Raisin Sauce (p.129)		•		•	
Orange & Red Wine Sauce (p.130)		•			
Passion Fruit Sauce (p.130)		•		•	
Maple Pecan Sauce (p.130)	•				•
Cooked Fruit Coulis (p.130)	•	•	•		
Fresh Fruit Coulis (p.130)	•	•	•		
Simple Chocolate Sauce (p.132)	•	•			•
White Chocolate Sauce (p.132)	•				
Fudge Sauce (p.132)	•		•		
Rich Fudge Sauce (p.132)	•		•		•
Nut Fudge Sauce (p.132)	•				•
Ginger Fudge Sauce (p.132)	•		•		
Brandy Fudge Sauce (p.132)	•				
Brandy Butter (p.133)			•	•	•
Rum & Ginger Butter (p.133)			•	•	•
Orange Butter (p.133)			•	•	•
Cherry Butter (p.133)			•	•	•

USEFUL ADDRESSES

BALDUCCI'S
424 Sixth Avenue
New York
NY 10011
Tel: 800-225-3822
www.balducci.com
Fine foods.

DEAN AND DELUCA
560 Broadway
New York
NY 10012
Tel: 800-221-7714
www.dean-deluca.com
Catalogue available. Fine foods
and specialty ingredients from
around the world.

FOODS OF INDIA
121 Lexington Avenue
New York
NY 10016
Tel: 212-683-4419
Spices, dried fruit, varieties
of rices and beans.

KITCHEN MARKET
218 Eigth Avenue
New York
NY 10011
Tel: 800-HOT-4433
Mexican and Southwestern foods.

MO-HOTTA-MO-BETTA
P.O. Box 4136
San Luis Obispo
CA 93403
Tel: 800-462-3220
Chilies etc.

PENZEY'S SPICES
P.O. Box 933
Muskego
WI 53150
Tel: 414-679-7207
www.penzys.com
Wide range of spices and herbs.

SPICE CORNER
135 Lexington Avenue
New York
NY 10016
Tel: 212-689-5182
Indian foods.

ZABARS
2245 Broadway
New York
NY 10024
Tel: 800-697-6301
zabars@infohouse.com
Fine foods.

INDEX

ACKNOWLEDGMENTS

Author's Appreciation
Writing a book such as *Sauces & Salsas* is a team effort and I would like to thank all who were involved in its creation. In the office: to Susannah Marriott who always has time for my moans but allows me the freedom (wherever possible) to express myself; to Tracey Ward, and to Nicky Graimes who, although did not work on the book, was involved in the original concept. Thanks go to my assistant Alison Austin who always stays calm; to Amanda Young, my angel, who inspired many of the Southeast Asian sauces; to Sue Storey, Jane Suthering, and Jane Middleton. Special thanks must go to Ian O'Leary whose unfailing patience, strong sense of humor and superb artistry brought life and vitality to the book, and to his assistant Emma Brogi; and finally to my editor Nasim Mawji whose enthusiasm, friendship, inquiring mind and intelligence made this book such a pleasure to write.

Dorling Kindersley would like to thank David Summers and Janice Anderson for editorial work; Bodum for the supply of pots and pans; Celia Morris at Kitchen Aid for supplying an electric mixer; The Fresh Olive Company for the supply of olive oil; Pam Bewley at Magimix for supplying a Magimix; Hujo's restaurant in Berwick Street. Thanks to Valerie Chandler for the index.

DK Publishing Inc. would like to thank Jane Perlmutter and Irene Pavitt for editorial input.